The Ultimate
John Wayne
Trivia Book

The Ultimate John Wayne Trivia Book

by Alvin H. Marill

A Citadel Press Book
Published by Carol Publishing Group

A Citadel Press Book
Published by Carol Publishing Group
Citadel Press is a registered trademark of Carol Communications, Inc.

Editorial, sales and distribution, rights and permissions inquiries
should be addressed Carol Publishing Group, 120 Enterprise Avenue,
    Secaucus, N.J. 07094

In Canada: Canadian Manda Group, One Atlantic Avenue, Suite 105,
    Toronto, Ontario M6K 3E7

Carol Publishing Group books may be purchased in bulk at special
discounts for sales promotions, fund-raising, or educational purposes.
Special editions can be created to specifications. For details, contact
Special Sales Department, 120 Enterprise Avenue, Secaucus, N.J. 07094

Manufactured in the United States of America
10 9 8 7 6 5 4 3 2

Library of Congress Cataloging-in-Publication Data

Marill, Alvin H.
    The ultimate John Wayne trivia book / Alvin H. Marill.
        p.   cm.
    "A Citadel Press book."
    ISBN 0-8065-1660-7 (pbk.)
    1. Wayne, John, 1907-1979—Miscellanea. I. Title.
    PN2287.W454M27 1995
    791.43'028'092—dc20   95-19765
                                                    CIP

Preface

DUKE. I like the sound of the word.

Paraphasing John Wayne's opening line of the immortal "Republic" monologue from *The Alamo*, his 1960 paean to the American dream of freedom and his encapsulating tribute to the West that once was, is a way of defining the riding tall and riding hard icon who became Mr. Movie Western during his fifty years on the screen (despite the fact that less than half his films were hoss operas).

Virtually all moviegoers of a particular age know John Wayne's movies. Buffs really know John Wayne's movies. Fanatics can cite chapter and verse. What follows is a collection of questions, a number of which are, I feel, real stumpers about the erstwhile Marion Michael Morrison of Winterset, Iowa, who went on to become John Wayne of Hollywood and finally simply, to fans, colleagues, the world—Duke.

How much do you, the reader, really know about John Wayne's movies? About

- His saddle pals—like who was his first *black* sidekick and in what film?
- His leading ladies—like what screen beauty hauled off and gave him a real haymaker in their only movie together?
- His on- and off-screen carousing buddies—like which chum acted with Wayne in more films than any other performer?

- His four-legged friends—like in how many of his films did his horse get costar billing, and who was that horse?

- His directors—like which rugged superstar director, known for working with the screen's he-men, called the shots on just two Wayne movies?

- His children—like in how many of his dad's films did son Michael act. Michael is now best known for producing many of the Duke's latter-day movies and is keeper of the Wayne flame.

- His screen utterances—like "Baby sister, I was born game," which came from what film?

- His movie promotions—like which of his films was promoted as "The Big One With the Big Two"?

- His screen women—like which actress was spanked by Wayne in one film and kicked in the rear by him in another?

- His unplanned replacements—like which Wayne films had him stepping in for previously scheduled Spencer Tracy, Glenn Ford, and Robert Mitchum?

- His screen pets—like who were Sam, Gabriel, Bananas, and Gen. Sterling Price?

- His musical talents—like which film had him singing Gilbert and Sullivan?

- His bushwackers—like who played the varmint who did Wayne in in his penultimate death on the screen?

- His barroom brawls—like which one took place in a woman's dress shop and which one in a British pub?

- His wars fought onscreen—like in which one was he *not* an officer but merely an enlisted man?

- His private lives and assorted wives—like what did the various Mrs. Waynes have in common?

And in what picture did Wayne kiss Walter Brennan?

You're gonna learn (or perhaps recall) the answers to all of these and hundreds more in *The Ultimate John Wayne Trivia Book,* pilgrim. But nothing comes easy. There's no pattern to these questions and answers. That would make it less difficult. These questions come from all phases of his career in scattershot fashion as if from the Wayne six-shooter or long gun.

For their assistance and encouragement, I have these colleagues to thank—for suggesting questions, offering ideas, providing photos, lending tapes, checking facts, and assuring the author of the fairness of each and every trivia query: in alphabetical order, Alan Barbour, John Cocchi, Allen Eyles, Lee Pfeiffer, and Jerry Vermilye.

So now Wayne-iacs, saddle up for the big five hundred and one—and put up your Duke!

The Ultimate
John Wayne
Trivia Book

In *Rooster Cogburn*

John Wayne Trivia Questions

Q1. "They outnumber us four to one. Do we talk or fight?" To whom did John Wayne pose this question—and in what film?

Q2. How many movies did Wayne make with director John Ford? Who was the runner-up?

Q3. Name eight Wayne films in which he played the character Stony Brooke.

Q4. What was the name of Wayne's dog in *Hondo* (1953)? In *North to Alaska* (1960)? In *Big Jake* (1971)?

Q5. John Wayne was responsible for protégé James Arness's getting the role of Marshal Matt Dillon in TV's *Gunsmoke*. Name the Wayne movies in which Arness was featured.

Q6. In the TV remake of what Wayne movie did James Arness have the Wayne role?

Q7. What were John Wayne's opening words in *Wake of the Red Witch* (1948)?

Q8. In *The Fighting Seabees* (1944), what was Wayne's job and what was the job of costar Susan Hayward?

Q9. What did Wayne do for a living in *A Man Betrayed* (1941) and why had he come to Temple City where the action takes place?

With Jean Arthur

Q10. How did Wayne meet leading lady Jean Arthur in *A Lady Takes a Chance* (1943)?

Q11. Name four football films in which Wayne appeared.

Q12. A barroom brawl was one element of a number of Wayne films. Name one that opened *and* closed with a barroom brawl.

Q13. What was Wayne's first film in color and what was his role?

Q14. Name the films in which Wayne (a) knocked down well-fires in Venezuela, (b) built a railroad tunnel through the Andes, (c) pillaged and roistered in ancient Mongolia, (d) helped infant Israel to statehood, (e) found himself downed as a pilot in the wastelands north of Labrador, (f) played a merchant marine in Hong Kong, and (g) hunted treasure in the Sahara.

Q15. Wayne was involved in memorable screen donnybrooks in *The Spoilers, The Quiet Man,* and *Tall in the Saddle.* With whom did he exchange fisticuffs in these films?

Q16. In what World War II–set film did John Wayne play (of all things) a "good German"?

Q17. What eighties movie pilfered the plot from a Wayne film of the forties and went on to win an Oscar for Best Original Screenplay?

Q18. Name seven post-*Stagecoach* films in which Wayne took second billing to his leading lady.

Q19. Which Wayne leading ladies later went on to win Oscars?

Q20. Name three literary works in the film versions of which Wayne appeared.

Q21. John Wayne costarred in a World War II movie that was written by a person whom Wayne portrayed in another film a decade later. What are the names of the two films?

Q22. Name three films produced by Wayne in which he starred and two in which he did not appear.

Q23. From what town did the stagecoach depart in John Ford's 1939 classic, where was it headed, and why was John Wayne as the Ringo Kid aboard?

Q24. Who was James Edward Grant?

Q25. Who scored the most John Wayne movies?

The cast of *Stagecoach: (from left)* Claire Trevor, John Wayne, Andy Devine, John Carradine, Louise Platt, Thomas Mitchell, Berton Churchill, Donald Meek, and George Bancroft

Q26. True or false: Except for "guest bits" in movies like *How the West Was Won, The Greatest Story Ever Told,* and several others, and gag walk-ons, Wayne always received top billing after 1945.

Q27. In how many films did Wayne appear with son Patrick, daughter Aissa, and son Michael? And on which John Wayne films was Michael billed as producer?

Q28. Who does not belong in this list: James Stewart, Robert Mitchum, Gary Cooper, Frank Sinatra, Randolph Scott, Jack Benny?

Q29. Which of these actresses never made a movie with John Wayne: Marlene Dietrich, Barbara Stanwyck, Bette Davis, Lana Turner, Joan Crawford, Katharine Hepburn, Lauren Bacall?

Q30. Name three Wayne movies for which the directors received Oscar nominations.

Q31. Wayne made more films for Republic than for any other studio. How many? What was the runner-up studio?

Q32. Although Maureen O'Hara is generally considered Wayne's most frequent leading lady, with which actress did he work most often?

Q33. *Sands of Iwo Jima* (1949) not only brought John Wayne his first Oscar nomination but also killed him off at the finale. How did he meet his end?

Q34. Where do we first find John Wayne in *Legend of the Lost* (1957)?

Q35. In *Tall in the Saddle,* the 1944 mystery Western, Wayne's character turns down the job of foreman at the KC ranch for what reason?

Q36. *Flame of Barbary Coast* (1945) was special for John Wayne for what reason?

Q37. Claire Trevor was billed over John Wayne in three consecutive pictures; name them.

Q38. What cinematographer photographed the most Wayne movies?

Q39. Name two John Wayne films with the same title.

Q40. In how many films did Wayne play a (different) character named John?

Q41. In the 1986 television remake of *Stagecoach,* who had the Wayne role of the Ringo Kid?

Q42. John Wayne became known as Duke (after the dog he owned when he was a young man). In which films was Duke the name of his character?

Q43. *Seven Sinners* from 1940 was the first of three movies in which John Wayne costarred with Marlene Dietrich. When the film was remade a decade later, Shelley Winters had Dietrich's role, but who had Wayne's?

Q44. Name seven real-life figures portrayed by John Wayne on the screen.

Q45. What six John Ford movies starring Wayne were shot in Monument Valley?

Q46. "Don't call me grandpappy, don't call me Methuselah, call me Ethan" was an admonition Wayne gave to whom in what film?

Q47. When *Three Godfathers* (1948) was remade for television (as *The Godchild*) in 1974, who played Wayne's role?

Q48. Aside from stuntmen Yakima Canutt and Chuck Roberson, who made thirty and twenty-seven films with Wayne, respectively, what actor worked with him most frequently?

Q49. Wayne acted in how many television dramas?

Q50. In *Three Faces West* (1940), how did Wayne and leading lady Sigrid Gurie meet?

Q51. Name the Wayne film in which the characters played by the four leads were formally named Samuel, James, William, and David.

Q52. In what film did Wayne give his horse a slap on the rump and his leading lady a slap across the face in the same scene? And what was the horse's name?

Q53. *The Spoilers* (1942), the second of three films in which Wayne's popularity was used to prop up Marlene Dietrich's wobbling film career, had already been filmed three times earlier and would later be made again. Who had the Wayne role in the other four versions of the Rex Beach tale?

Q54. Name three Wayne pictures that were set *before* the American Revolution.

Q55. How did Wayne and John Ford meet?

Q56. How did John Wayne happen to become the star of *Blood Alley* (1955), the first venture of his newly created Batjac production company?

The Duke with Pappy (John Ford)

Q57. Wayne was the captain of what ship in DeMille's *Reap the Wild Wind* (1942) and how did he happen to meet leading lady Paulette Goddard?

Q58. Two television series were based on two Wayne movies but he wasn't in either of them. What are the titles of the two series, and who played the Wayne role in each?

Q59. In what two films did Wayne act with a British "Sir" (once and future)?

Q60. What battle is the backdrop for John Ford's Civil War sequence in *How the West Was Won* (1962) involving John Wayne and Harry Morgan as Generals Sherman and Grant?

Q61. John Wayne and Dean Martin were two of *The Sons of Katie Elder* in the 1965 Henry Hathaway Western. Who were the other two?

Q62. Who played Wayne's grandson in George Sherman's *Big Jake* (1971)?

Q63. Glen Campbell and Kim Darby were Wayne's costars in *True Grit* (1969). Name one other picture in which the two worked together, along with Joe Namath.

Q64. What was John Wayne's character name in the twelve-part 1933 Mascot serial, *The Three Musketeers*?

Q65. What was Roman centurion John Wayne's single line of dialogue in his less-than-three-minute role in *The Greatest Story Ever Told* (1965)?

Q66. Max von Sydow, of course, played Christ in *The Greatest Story Ever Told* in which Wayne did a walk-on as a Roman centurion. In what other film did the Duke appear with a future screen-Christ?

With Max Von Sydow as Christ

Q67. In *Angel and the Badman* (1947), Wayne was asked by costar Gail Russell how he got his name, Quirt Evans. What was his story?

Q68. In *The Fighting Kentuckian* (1949), where and when was the action set, what was Wayne's specific role as the title character, and what unlikely performer played his sidekick?

Q69. What was John Wayne's memorable line to sultry Lana Turner in *The Sea Chase* and to spirited Susan Hayward in *The Conqueror,* and what two other films did he and Hayward do together?

Q70. John Wayne's horse during the latter part of the Duke's career was named Dollor. Name six Westerns in which Wayne and Dollor teamed up.

Q71. True or false: John Wayne wore a mustache on the screen for the first time in John Ford's famed late-1940s Cavalry trilogy that began with *Fort Apache* and continued with *She Wore a Yellow Ribbon* and *Rio Grande.*

Q72. Name the first Wayne World War II–era movie that found him in uniform and name the last.

Q73. Wayne made his screen breakthrough in Raoul Walsh's *The Big Trail* in 1930. Which of these other "Trails" did he not take in the thirties?: *The Oregon Trail, The Lonely Trail, The Trail Beyond, Trail of the Lonesome Pine, Sagebrush Trail, The Desert Trail.*

Q74. What roles did Wayne and costar Patricia Neal play in both *Operation Pacific* (1951) and *In Harm's Way* (1965)?

Q75. What was John Wayne's final line of dialogue in *The Searchers* (1956)?

Q76. Name two Wayne movies in which Lauren Bacall was the leading lady.

Q77. In *Lady for a Night* (1941), what was the title of the book gambler John Wayne gave to costar Joan Blondell, riverboat owner and society wannabe, and what was the name of the gambling casino they owned together?

Q78. What Wayne movie featured both Harry Carey Sr. and Harry Carey Jr., and which Wayne picture was dedicated to the memory of Harry Carey Sr.? What was the screen dedication?

Q79. In what two films did Wayne spend some time as a deep sea diver?

Q80. Over his career, Wayne was a football player in several films and a boxer in a couple of others. In which one did he show he was a good skate as a hockey player?

Q81. In *New Frontier* (the second one), Wayne made his final appearance as one of the Three Mesquiteers and his leading lady made her film debut. Who was she? Name her only other picture in which she used that name (her real one).

Q82. What is the only picture in which Wayne worked with the onetime Leonard Slye?

Q83. True or false: John Wayne had his own series of comic books.

Q84. Name the movie in which John Wayne first captained a ship. Name the last.

Q85. Wayne's film production company, formed in the 1950s, was Batjac. Where did the name come from?

Q86. Name the Wayne film in which he told his leading lady (who proposed to him), "Sure I'll marry you only if you promise to sew on my buttons and cook my meals and darn my socks."

Q87. What was the name of the submarine Wayne commanded in *Operation Pacific* (1951)?

Wayne as Davy Crockett and Richard Widmark as Jim Bowie

Q88. John Wayne portrayed Davy Crockett in *The Alamo* (1960). Name five other actors who've played Davy Crockett on the screen.

Q89. Wayne was once cast as a singing cowboy named Singin' Sandy in *Riders of Destiny* (1933). Who dubbed him?

Q90. What was the only film Wayne made on location in Britain? What was his job? Where did the climactic shoot-out take place?

Q91. What were the names and nationalities of John Wayne's three wives?

Q92. What was the title character's full name in Wayne's *McQ* (1974)? Where was it filmed? Who played his boss?

Q93. In what Wayne films were his leading ladies named Eula Goodnight, Loxi Claiborne, Molly Truesdale, Pilar Graile, Flaxen Tarry, Angelique Desaix, and Fleurette DeMarchand?

Q94. How many Westerns did Wayne make and how many films in a modern setting?

Q95. Name the first movie in which Wayne appeared that got an Oscar nomination.

Q96. What was the title of the film in which the onetime Marion Morrison starred opposite the onetime Jeanette Morrison?

Q97. Name the Wayne movies that used these tag lines in their advertising: (1) "First she was afraid he'd stay— then she was afraid he wouldn't . . ." (2) "It's the Big One With the Big Two!" (3) "The Big Men Clash—and Nothing Can Match Them! The Big Men Ride—and Nothing Can Stop Them!"

Q98. Name the film and the recipient of this immortal bit of Wayne badinage: "You're comfy without the french fries."

Q99. In what film did Wayne costar with a future two-time United States ambassador, and in what film did he costar with the wife of a United States ambassador?

Q100. Name the film in which Wayne gave this "gung ho" speech: "This is the way it's gonna be. I'm a man. You're boys. Not cowmen, not by a damn sight. You're nothing but cow-*boys*. And I'm gonna remind you of that every minute of the day and night, across four hundred miles of the meanest country in the West. You'll get the best food in the territory, no rest, damn little sleep, and fifty silver dollars . . . if we get there." And what was significant about the ad campaign?

Q101. Of what Wayne film did one critic write, "It never Waynes, it bores"?

Q102. Name two post-*Stagecoach* Wayne films that had title changes shortly after their release.

Q103. "Fill yer hand, you sonofabitch" was the immortal line from what Wayne movie?

Q104. Who sang the title song to *The Man Who Shot Liberty Valance* (1962)?

Q105. *Chisum* (1970) received what kind of dubious distinction?

Q106. Dimitri Tiomkin scored what John Wayne movies?

Q107. Name the Wayne films that received Academy Award nominations for Best Picture.

Q108. Howard Hawks initially had envisioned what actors to play the *Red River* (1948) roles ultimately enacted by John Wayne and John Ireland?

Q109. Who was the man who shot Liberty Valance in the Wayne film of that name, and who played bad guy Valance?

Q110. What kind of credit did John Ford take on Robert Montgomery (he got top billing) and John Wayne's *They Were Expendable* (1945)?

Q111. Name four teen rock idols who acted opposite Wayne beginning in the late fifties.

Q112. At his death in 1979, how many grandchildren did Wayne have?

Q113. "There's some things a man just can't run away from" is a noted line John Wayne spoke in what film?

Q114. "In this movie several tons of dynamite are set off— none of it under the right people," onetime *Time* magazine critic James Agee noted sarcastically. What was the Wayne movie?

Q115. What Wayne movie had him dallying with his leading lady on the uninhabited although fictional South Seas island of Pom Pom Galli, and what contemporary star's father directed the film?

Q116. "You've seen the Duke in action . . . now watch him lose his temper!" was the advertising tag line to what Wayne movie? And what incongruous scene highlighted that ad campaign?

Q117. What two Westerns did Wayne make for the short-lived Cinema Center Films and who were his directors?

Q118. In Nicholas Ray's *Flying Leathernecks* (1951), what fighter squadron did Wayne take over at the beginning of the film and what were his opening remarks to his men?

Q119. In one of the few *Flying Leathernecks* scenes with his stateside wife, played by Janis Carter, Wayne displayed his affection with what comment?

Q120. What is the name given to the stolen paddlewheel ferry that Wayne pilots in William Wellman's *Blood Alley* (1955) and who is Wayne's rather incongruous first mate?

Q121. As *Blood Alley* begins, where do we find John Wayne and to whom is he talking?

Q122. "Our law is written by the wind and the dust" is a line from what modern-day Wayne Western involving émigrés from Hitler's Europe? Who was the leading lady and who was the director?

Q123. Who played Tucson Smith and Lullaby Joslin to Wayne's Stony Brooke in the first six 1939–40 "Three Mesquiteers" movies, who directed them all, and who replaced the Joslin character (now called Rusty) in the final two?

Q124. In what movie did Wayne dress down a fellow officer by calling him a "schoolboy" who "would expose himself and his men like you did this morning . . . This is a dirty war we're fighting [and] we've gotta fight it the right way," and then tell the soldier he's putting him in for the Distinguished Service Cross?

Q125. What actress was hired to coach Wayne on his "authentic" Swedish accent in *The Long Voyage Home*?

Q126. In Wayne's first starring role, who was his leading lady, and what other Wayne film was she also in?

Q127. Name a film with veteran Western star Jack Holt in which Wayne appeared, a Wayne film years later in which Holt had a small supporting role, and a film in which Wayne costarred with Tim Holt, his son.

Q128. What movie, advertised as "All Wayne and a World Wide," had him playing "the two-fisted boss of a three-ringed traveling Wild West show"?

As the Swede in the O'Neill adaptation

Q129. Name the vessel on which Wayne and company were sailing in Eugene O'Neill's *The Long Voyage Home* (1940). Name the one in *The Sea Chase* (1955).

Q130. In Wayne's first Mascot serial, *Shadow of the Eagle* (1932), what did he do for a living? In the second, *The*

Hurricane Express (1932)? In the third, *The Three Musketeers* (1933)?

Q131. In *El Dorado* (1967), Wayne was teamed with Robert Mitchum. Name the films in which he appeared with Mitchum's two acting sons.

Q132. Who played the outlaw leader being tracked by Texas Ranger Wayne in *The Comancheros* (1961), and who directed it, and who starred in the (unofficial) remake?

Q133. True or false: In Henry Hathaway's *The Shepherd of the Hills* (1941), Wayne had the title role.

Q134. George "Gabby" Hayes, filmdom's perennial cowboy sidekick, first worked with Wayne in what movie? What was their last film together?

With Gabby Hayes in *The Man From Utah* (1934)

Q135. John Agar made his movie debut in *Fort Apache* (where he acted with wife Shirley Temple). Name five other Wayne films in which he appeared.

Q136. What were the only two musicals in which Wayne appeared?

Q137. Name the Wayne films in which he acted with the performers who at other times portrayed fictional detectives Philip Marlowe, Mike Hammer, and Nero Wolfe.

Q138. Name the varmint who put a bullet in the Duke's back in the penultimate reel of *The Cowboys* (1972).

Q139. How did Wayne pass himself off to the initially hostile Lauren Bacall when they first met in *The Shootist* (1976) and what compliment did he later give her, similar to the one he gave to Susan Hayward in *The Conqueror* (1956)?

Q140. Name the forties films in which John Wayne took *third* billing to the same two costars.

Q141. With whom does Wayne duke it out in *Chisum*? In *The Undefeated*? In *The Quiet Man*? In *Sands of Iwo Jima*? In *Legend of the Lost*?

Q142. In *Rooster Cogburn* (1975), where did the action take place, why did Wayne lose his badge, and for how long was he "in service of the court"?

Q143. In what film were Wayne and his he-man costar, according to the ads, "the raiders on horseback who rode like thunder . . . and struck like lightning"? Who was the fellow rider? And what is significant about the movie in the director's canon?

Q144. At the start of *Blood Alley* (1955) when finding a surprise in a mattress delivered to him in his Red Chinese jail cell, what was Wayne's comment? And how did he manage to escape?

Q145. Lee Marvin played Liberty Valance in the Wayne film with that name in the title. Who played Cherry Valance in an earlier Wayne Western?

Q146. In *Without Reservations* (1946), what is the name of the book written by author Claudette Colbert that has Wayne's likeness on the cover? Also under what title did the film go into production initially?

Q147. Wayne, of course, played Rooster Cogburn on the screen twice. Who stepped into his big boots in the 1978 TV pilot movie based on Duke's two films?

Q148. In *Big Jake* (1971), to whom does Wayne bark: "You can call me father, you can call me Jacob, you can call me Jake, you can call me a dirty sonofabitch. But if you call me 'Daddy' again, I'll finish this fight."

Q149. How many Tennesseans were under Wayne's command as Davy Crockett in *The Alamo* (1960)?

Q150. Over his career, Wayne fought in various American wars through Vietnam. In what film did he fight in Korea?

Q151. "You're going to wind up staggering into your bunk every night with your hip pocket draggin'. Then you'll lay there lookin' at the ceiling while your stomach turns over and you hope to God you called every shot right during the day. The next morning you'll wake up and wish you were a flight lieutenant again, so all you'd have to do is what the man told you. And you'll get bad-tempered and snarly just like me. You'll probably wind up just like me. Climbin' into an aircraft with your hip pockets draggin', you'll go back to some desk job. Brother, I didn't do you any favor." This is Wayne's farewell speech to whom in what movie?

Q152. Although Barbra Streisand and John Wayne were poles apart politically, how did their paths happen to cross?

As Lt. Col. Benjamin Vandervoot in Darryl F. Zanuck's 1962 epic

Q153. Wayne was in what two films shot in Cinerama?

Q154. Although most major films after the mid-fifties were shot in color, what two John Wayne pictures of the sixties, made back to back, were in black and white?

Q155. What was unique about John Wayne's billing in *The Longest Day* (1962)?

Q156. Which of the following titles was not that of a Wayne movie: *The Man From Utah, Men Are Like That, The Man From Monterey, Men Without Women, The Man From Colorado?*

Q157. What noted Mexican actor costarred with Wayne in three movies?

Q158. In *Wake of the Red Witch* (1948), who played Mayrant Ruysdaal Sidneye, tyrannical head of a trading empire and owner of the title vessel? And who played Wayne's first mate in the film?

Q159. Natalie Wood played the teenager Wayne set out to rescue from her kidnappers in *The Searchers* (1956). Who had the part of the girl as a youngster when she was taken?

Q160. Prolific composers Johnny Mercer and Hoagy Carmichael wrote the song "Just for Tonight" for what John Wayne movie?

Q161. Name the Wayne film that was advertised with these words: "Battling it out toe to toe and side by side across two thousand miles of thundering adventure! They feared no one—Juarista rebels, cutthroat Banditos, the armies of Maximilian . . . as they challenged an angry land—and each other!" Who costarred and who directed?

Q162. Name the rooster that became Wayne's "alarm clock" in *Blood Alley.*

Q163. In *The Quiet Man* (1952), how did John Wayne happen to turn up in Ireland?

Q164. Name twelve professional athletes who acted in Wayne movies.

Q165. In what Wayne movie did Barry Fitzgerald costar and in what film did Fitzgerald's brother Arthur Shields appear?

Early 1930s Wayne in black tie with Loretta Young

Q166. Wayne's leading lady in *Three Girls Lost* (1931) was
Loretta Young. In what picture did he costar with her
older sister and in what picture did he appear with
their (much later) brother-in-law?

Q167. In *Island in the Sky* (1953), for whom did Wayne work?
Who played his buddy/confidant and functioned in the
same role opposite the Duke in a later film?

Q168. Two Wayne movie colleagues and drinking buddies were Ward Bond and Victor McLaglen. How many of the Duke's films did each of them do? And how many Wayne films did Andrew McLaglen (Victor's son) direct?

Q169. Wayne costarred with Kirk Douglas in what three films?

With Kirk Douglas

Q170. In *McLintock!* (1963), what was Wayne's full name? In *True Grit* (1969)?

Q171. What military rank did Wayne hold in the following movies: (1) *They Were Expendable;* (2) *Fort Apache;* (3) *Sands of Iwo Jima;* (4) *She Wore a Yellow Ribbon;* (5) *Rio Grande;* (6) *Flying Leathernecks;* (7) *Jet Pilot;* (8) *The Alamo;* (9) *The Longest Day;* (10) *In Harm's Way;* (11) *Cast a Giant Shadow;* (12) *The Green Berets;* (13) *Back to Bataan;* (14) *Operation Pacific;* (15) *The Wings of Eagles;* (16) *The Horse Soldiers;* (17) *How the West Was Won?*

Q172. What was the name of Wayne's horse in *A Lady Takes a Chance* (1943) and his mule in *Legend of the Lost* (1957)?

Q173. In *Three Godfathers* (1948), what was the full name of John Wayne's character? And what was his occupation?

Q174. Who played Philadelphia Thursday in the Wayne movie *Fort Apache*? Teleia Van Schreeven in *Wake of the Red Witch*? Sabra Cameron in *A Man Betrayed*? Jersey Thomas in *Dakota*? Abby Allshard in *She Wore a Yellow Ribbon*? Shasta Delaney in *Rio Lobo*? Amelia Dedham in *Donovan's Reef*?

Q175. When Wayne takes a final salute from his men in *She Wore a Yellow Ribbon* (1949), he is given a solid silver watch as a retirement gift. What is the engraved sentiment?

Q176. Several of John Wayne's fellow players in *The Shootist* (1976) starred in television series. Name four of them.

Q177. In *The Train Robbers* (1973), Ricardo Montalban played the role of The Pinkerton Man (as he was billed). Which of Wayne's longtime buddies was to have had the part?

Q178. Henry Fonda was Wayne's military superior in what three films?

Q179. Dimitri Tiomkin wrote the score to the John Wayne movie *The High and the Mighty*. Who had a Top Ten recording of the popular main theme in the summer of 1954?

Q180. Lee Marvin gave John Wayne what bit of advice in *The Comancheros* (1961)?

Q181. What was the name of the deceased wife of Wayne's character in *She Wore a Yellow Ribbon*?

Q182. Wayne played big-game catcher Sean Mercer in Africa in Howard Hawks's *Hatari!* (1962). What does the title mean?

Q183. *Cast a Giant Shadow* (1966) was filmed on location in Israel, but where were "special guest" John Wayne's scenes shot?

Q184. "I never feel sorry for anything that happens to a woman" was Wayne's philosophy in what forties movie?

Q185. Wayne was the star of *Three Faces West* (1940), and Frances Dee was the leading lady in *Four Faces West* (1948). In between, what film did they appear in together?

Q186. Among the many name actors who joined Wayne in *The Longest Day* was pop singer Paul Anka (playing a U.S. ranger). What other credit did he have in that film?

Q187. Name at least two films in which Wayne turned his leading lady over his knee for a good spanking.

Q188. "I always forgive a lady one murder" was a Wayne line to whom in what adventure film?

With Marguerite Churchill in his first major film

Q189. Who played Wayne leading lady Vera Ralston's father in their two films together?

Q190. Veteran director Raoul Walsh directed Wayne's first significant picture, *The Big Trail* (1930). What was the only other Walsh-Wayne screen collaboration?

Q191. Name the never-realized film Wayne was supposed to have made for Sam Fuller in 1955 with Tyrone Power and Ava Gardner as his costars.

Q192. Which Wayne movie was initially to have had Glenn Ford in Duke's part and which was to have had Spencer Tracy?

Q193. After being wounded in the climactic shoot-out with bad guy George Kennedy and cohorts in *Cahill, United States Marshal* (1973), what advice did Wayne give his two teenage sons who got involved with the varmints? And how was Wayne's character wounded?

Q194. Under what name did the Wayne character box in *The Quiet Man*?

Q195. How did Wayne meet leading lady Ella Raines in *Tall in the Saddle* (1944)?

With Ella Raines for the only time

Q196. In *She Wore a Yellow Ribbon,* what are the opening three words intoned by the narrator? How does this create a significant plot blooper?

Q197. *San Timoteo* was the original production title of what seventies Wayne movie?

Q198. An impatient Wayne groused "Rhinos, buffalo, elephants, and a greenhorn" about whom in *Hatari!* (1962)?

Q199. In *Fort Apache* (1948), how many men did Wayne take with him to talk to Cochise? And what were Wayne's first words to the legendary Indian leader?

Q200. When advised that "We're giving you an absolutely free hand," Wayne responded to whom (and in what movie), "Then you'd better shake it. Because I'm leaving right now"? And in what other picture did the two work together?

Q201. In *The Maltese Falcon,* Bogart's memorable line was about "the stuff dreams are made of." Wayne used that very line in what film, and to what was he referring?

Q202. After he became a major star, what were the only two studios for which John Wayne did not make a movie?

Q203. Name three films in which Wayne took a mud bath, engaging in all-out brawls in muddy cowtown streets.

Q204. How many years had Wayne's character put in the military at his retirement, what did he plan to do after leaving, and what convinced him to stay at the fade-out of *She Wore a Yellow Ribbon*?

Q205. "I'm lookin' at a tin star with a drunk pinned to it" was Duke's observation in what film?

Q206. What was "The Wayne Reporter"?

Q207. Name the character played by Wayne in *Tall in the Saddle.*

Q208. Six years after starring in *True Grit,* Wayne reprised his role as the fat, boozing, one-eyed marshal in *Rooster Cogburn.* Name the one costar who also appeared in both films (although in different roles).

Q209. In the first of John Ford's cavalry trilogy, *Fort Apache,* and in the third, *Rio Grande,* Wayne played two separate characters using (more or less) the same name. He was Capt. Kirby York in the former, Lt. Col. Kirby Yorke (with a final *e*) in the latter. In the second, *She Wore a Yellow Ribbon,* and the third, Ben Johnson and Victor McLaglen played the same characters. What were their names?

Q210. What one John Wayne movie later came to the musical stage and who had Wayne's role in it?

Q211. Name a film that had both John Wayne and Mickey Rooney in the cast—both minor parts, although the Mick's role was somewhat larger than the Duke's.

Q212. Name the film in which Wayne came up with a line like "Monsoor—you are a lulu!"

Q213. In Wayne's 1934 Lone Star Western for Monogram, *West of the Divide,* George Hayes (he wasn't "Gabby" yet) played a cowpoke named Dusty Rhodes. He also played a totally different character called Dusty in what other Wayne Lone Star?

Q214. Wayne romanced his leading lady in what film with such lines as "You've got the most beautiful eyes in South America . . . and a cute little nose, too!"?

Q215. In *The Desert Trail* (1935), one of his Lone Star Westerns that managed to have a telephone on the wall and a leading lady in modern (thirties) dress and heels, Wayne was headed from what town to what town?

Settling a disagreement with Lee Marvin

Q216. Welcome, Arizona, was the cowtown in which Wayne found himself at both the beginning and end of what film?

Q217. In what three films did Wayne and Lee Marvin engage in fisticuffs?

Q218. Wayne had the title role in *McLintock!*, but in what Wayne film did his old friend and mentor Harry Carey Sr. costar as a character named McLintock (first name: Wistful)?

Q219. From what Wayne film did this inspiring speech come: "We always remember the Thursdays, but what of the others? They aren't forgotten because they haven't died. They're living—right out there . . . They'll keep on living as long as the regiment lives. Their pay is thirteen dollars a month, their diet beans and hay. Maybe horsemeat before this campaign is over. They'll fight over rotgut and whiskey but share the last drop in their canteens. The faces may change . . . the names . . . but they're there. They're the regiment—the regular army. Now and fifty years from now. They're better men than they used to be. Thursday did it. He made it a command to be proud of."

Q220. Impressionists invariably use the word "pilgrim" when doing John Wayne. Name two films in which Wayne actually called someone a pilgrim.

Q221. In *Riders of Destiny* (1933), "John Wayne as 'Singin' Sandy' " (as he was billed above the title) was first seen in the opening of his first Lone Star Western doing what?

Q222. Wayne in top hat stepped up to the bar at the start of *In Old California* (1942) and ordered what?

Q223. What is the legend inscribed on the congressional medal awarded posthumously to the Duke?

Q224. In *The Shootist,* on what day did Wayne, as John Bernard Books, ride into Carson City, Nevada, and what was his first stop?

Q225. Where did John Wayne and Randolph Scott have their slugfest in *Pittsburgh* (1942)? In *The Spoilers* (1942)?

Q226. What regiment did John Wayne lead in *The Horse Soldiers* (1959) and what was his job before the war?

Q227. In *Haunted Gold* (1932), one of Wayne's six low-budget Warner Bros. Westerns, who played Duke's sidekick, where did he battle the bad guy, and who played the Wayne role in the original (silent) version called *The Phantom City*?

Q228. What was Rooster Cogburn's response in *True Grit* when teenager Mattie Ross (Kim Darby) asked him if he was "still game" about going after her dad's killer?

Q229. Wayne starred in five films for Metro-Goldwyn-Mayer. Name them.

Q230. Where is the structure that has been restored and designated "The Birthplace of John Wayne"?

Q231. In his first picture after *The Big Trail* (1930), what was Wayne's role and what was the title of the film?

Q232. *Dark Command* (1940) was the only film Wayne made with Roy Rogers. What was Wayne's only film with Dale Evans?

Q233. What latter-day John Wayne Western began life as a play by Hungarian playwright Laszlo Fodor?

Q234. How was the knockdown fight between John Wayne and Ward Bond ended in *The Shepherd of the Hills* (1941)?

Q235. In what three films did Wayne have it out with Richard Boone?

Q236. "I don't know much about thoroughbreds, horses, or women. Them that I did know I never liked. They're too nervous and spooky; they scare me. But you're one high-bred filly that don't. 'Course I don't know what you're talkin' about half the time. But it don't matter. Bein' around you pleases me." In what movie did Wayne give this roundabout declaration of love?

Q237. Who was Wayne's drinking buddy in both *True Grit* and *Rooster Cogburn*?

With Henry Fonda and Shirley Temple in *Fort Apache*

Q238. *Marihuana,* which had absolutely nothing to do with the plant, was the German title of what John Wayne movie?

Q239. John Wayne played Pittsburgh in *Pittsburgh,* Elsa Martinelli played Dallas in *Hatari!,* and Shirley Temple was Philadelphia in Wayne's *Fort Apache.* In the last film, where did Temple say she was born?

Q240. In what film, which costarred his son Pat, featured his young daughter Aissa, and was produced by his son Michael, did Wayne, according to the advertising campaign, "like his whiskey hard . . . his women soft . . . and his West all to himself"?

Q241. Many familiar character actors did comic relief in Wayne movies using unusual monickers. Name the Wayne movie in which (1) Edgar Buchanan played an Injun called Bunny Dull; (2) Andy Devine was Link Appleyard; (3) William Frawley was Wolf Wylie; (4) Phil Silvers was Smiley Lambert; (5) George "Gabby" Hayes was Desprit Dean; (6) Shemp Howard was Shorty the Tailor; (7) John Fiedler was J. Noble Daggett; (8) Grant Withers was Whanger Spreckles.

Q242. "Republic. I like the sound of the word!" This line began one of Wayne's familiar monologues in *The Alamo* (1960). In Republic's first movie, *Westward Ho* (1935), Wayne (presumably dubbed) "sang" what song to heroine Sheila Manners (later Sheila Bromley) under a prairie moon?

Q243. In *Rooster Cogburn,* Wayne explained to Katharine Hepburn how he happened to lose his left eye. What happened? And what was earlier his explanation to Kim Darby in *True Grit*?

Q244. Wayne did a gag walk-on in Bob Hope's *Cancel My Reservation* (1972), as Hope imagines he is to be hanged. What was the Duke's one line of dialogue?

Q245. In *In Old California* (1942), Wayne was a druggist, as his real life dad had been. What was his role in *California Straight Ahead* (1937)?

Q246. In what film was Wayne's character praised as "the only guy I know who had guts enough not to commit suicide"? Name three things about the picture that were significant to Wayne's career.

Q247. Name the Wayne movies in which Brian Donlevy played the sinister Trader Callendar and John Carradine portrayed the nasty Ulrich Windler.

Q248. Tim McCoy and Buck Jones were major cowboy stars during Wayne's early days in films. Name at least one picture he did with each.

Q249. Name five movies starring John Wayne that had their world premieres at Radio City Music Hall in New York.

Q250. "That'll teach 'em to monkey with construction men!" was Wayne's statement after what action in what wartime flag-waver?

Q251. It was Errol Flynn who starred in the Western *Dodge City* in 1939, but where was the Dodge City where John Wayne found himself in charge?

Q252. At the opening of *The Shootist,* while clips from some of his best-known Westerns were being shown, Wayne, in voiceover, gave his character's credo. What was it?

Q253. Vera Miles costarred with Wayne as his niece in what film? As his fiancée in what film? As his wife in what two films?

Q254. How much does Wayne charge Kim Darby in *True Grit* to go after her father's killer?

Q255. Admiring barefoot Betty Field in her tight jeans as she hefts sacks of flour, what remark does John Wayne utter in *The Shepherd of the Hills* (1941)?

Q256. Name the Wayne films that had these tag lines as their advertising come-ons:
(1) "A go-get-'em guy for the U.S.A. on a terror-trail that leads half-a-world away!"
(2) "The story of a babe, a bully, and a brawl!"
(3) "Wayne at his mightiest! Adventure at its best!"
(4) "No man can pay the price for what this woman offers!"

(5) "The daredevil who actually parlayed fourteen dollars, a pair of crutches, and a redhead's love into world fame!"

Q257. In what film did Wayne and one of the two leading ladies swap billing with the two "stars" when it was reissued sometime after its initial release?

Q258. Albert Dekker was the varmint making things rough for Wayne in what two similarly titled forties' movies?

Q259. In *Chisum* (1970), what was John Wayne's response just before the fadeout to sidekick Ben Johnson's observation that "There's an old sayin'—there's no law west of Dodge and no God west of the Pecos"?

Q260. Wayne's young daughter Aissa appeared in what three films with him?

Q261. Wayne's seafaring character dreamed of home in *The Long Voyage Home* (1940). How long had it been, did he say, since he'd seen his mother and how did he express his thoughts in broken English?

Q262. On the ads for *Jet Pilot* (1957), who got third billing after John Wayne and Janet Leigh?

Q263. Who did the voice-over narration during the opening credits of *Chisum,* who sang the main song, and what was distinctive about the way the film was set up?

Q264. For what studios did Wayne make *Rio Grande, Rio Bravo, Rio Lobo,* and *Rio Conchos*?

Q265. In *Rio Grande* (1950), what was Wayne's soldierly advice to his son, played by Claude Jarman Jr., about the army when he suddenly found the boy in his command?

Q266. Wayne's second teaming with Donna Reed, following John Ford's *They Were Expendable* (1945), was in Michael Curtiz's little-seen *Trouble Along the Way*

(1953). He was a former big-time football coach now coaching for a small Catholic college. What did she do for a living?

Q267. While he was Republic Pictures' leading leading man of the forties, Wayne had as his costar Gail Russell in what two movies and Vera Ralston in what two?

Q268. In what war movie was Robert Ryan Wayne's subordinate and in what one was he Wayne's superior?

Q269. What pictures did perennial cowboy sidekick Walter Brennan make with John Wayne?

Q270. Wayne made three consecutive Westerns in 1932 that had been filmed before by cowboy star Ken Maynard. Name them.

Q271. In John Ford's *Stagecoach* (1939), he was one of Wayne's traveling companions and in John Ford's *The Long Voyage Home* (1940), he was one of Wayne's shipmates (although he had third billing, he was actually the star). Who was he?

Q272. What musical theme interpolated into the Richard Hageman score for *The Long Voyage Home* became a jukebox hit a decade later?

Q273. In what film did Wayne costar with two single-named actors, in what year did it take place, and where did he meet his leading lady in the movie?

Q274. What real-life figure who was a relatively minor character in Ford's *The Horse Soldiers* with whom Wayne discussed military strategy, did Wayne later play in two other ventures with Ford?

Q275. Name five Wayne leading ladies who starred on Broadway in musical comedies.

Q276. Wayne dukes it out with Forrest Tucker at the climax of *Chisum*. In what other film did they appear together, and what two other actors were in both movies?

Duking it out with Montgomery Clift in *Red River* . . .

Bruce Cabot in *The Undefeated* . . .

Rock Hudson in *The Undefeated* . . .

and Forrest Tucker in *Chisum*

Q277. How did Wayne once describe one of his most infamous films, *The Conqueror*?

Q278. In *The Fighting Kentuckian* (1949), how did Wayne ingratiate himself to leading lady Vera Ralston?

Q279. In what film is Wayne described this way by one of the cast members: "He's all Navy and nothing but Navy"?

Q280. Name the film in which John Wayne played a guide named Joe January.

Q281. In the early days of sound, films were often shot simultaneously in several languages. Such was the case of Raoul Walsh's *The Big Trail* (1930), in which Wayne had his first starring role. Who played Wayne's part in the French, Spanish, Italian, and German versions, all made at the same time (with different directors) using the same sets?

With Ona Munson in *Lady From Louisiana*

Q282. What three films had the prominent billing "A John Wayne Production"?

Q283. "We both believe in uplifting the masses" was a laugh-inducing Wayne line from what less-than-memorable film?

Q284. What was unusual about *A Man Betrayed* and *Lady From Louisiana,* Wayne's two back-to-back 1941 movies for Republic, released less than a month apart?

Q285. Where is John Wayne Airport and where is John Wayne Elementary School?

Q286. Who created the western paintings displayed during the opening credits of *El Dorado*?

Q287. What three Wayne movies were scored by Max Steiner?

Q288. The John Wayne character died onscreen in what eight movies?

Q289. George Kennedy was a lowdown varmint who lost the big shoot-out with Wayne in both *The Sons of Katie Elder* (1965) and *Cahill, United States Marshal* (1973). In what movie was he Wayne's military superior?

Q290. In what Western did Wayne's character have a side-kick/confidant named Jebediah Nightlinger?

Q291. "Not thinkin' . . . just remembrin' " was a Wayne line in what film?

Q292. About which Wayne movie did *Time* magazine complain, "The film lasts almost as long as five TV Westerns laid end to end—and makes about as little consecutive sense . . ."?

Q293. Name the Wayne movie in which a running joke about a pair of crutches involved a significant movie blooper.

Q294. In *The Sons of Katie Elder,* elder son Wayne quotes the opening page of the family Bible. What does it say?

And how did his father die, causing Duke and his "brothers" to seek vengeance?

Q295. Jeremy Slate played the "conscientious" deputy sheriff, Dennis Hopper the sniveling son of the town kingpin, and Strother Martin a saloon barfly in *The Sons of Katie Elder* with the Duke. They all appeared again in what other Wayne movie?

Q296. *The War Wagon* (1967) cast John Wayne and Kirk Douglas as friendly rivals. When the two gun down a pair of bushwackers, Douglas boasted, "Mine hit the ground first!" What was Wayne's response?

Q297. Alfred, Lionel, and Emil Newman were among the great film scorers during the Golden Age of Hollywood. Name at least one John Wayne movie each did.

Q298. What was unusual about John Wayne's appearance at Harvard in 1974 to accept his Man of the Year award?

Q299. In *The Green Berets* (1968), what did gruff but compassionate commander Wayne tell the concerned Vietnamese waif who had become the mascot of Dodge City?

Q300. Where does the famous seven-ton, twenty-one-foot-high bronze sculpture of John Wayne on horseback and in cowboy gear stand?

Q301. What did Wayne order inscribed on his tombstone in *The Shootist,* and how did he arrive at the Metropole saloon where he would meet his fate?

Q302. Name five Caucasian actors who played unlikely Native Americans in Wayne movies.

Q303. Dimitri Tiomkin and Ned Washington, who gave the world "High Noon," wrote the title song to Wayne's movie *The War Wagon* (1967). Who sang the song under the opening titles?

Q304. What Wayne film alternately used these headlines as come-ons: "GUILTY of Daring to Love and Live!" and "They found a haven of refuge in a new land—and a haven of love in each other's arms!" and what was Duke's role in it?

Q305. In Wayne's *Chisum,* nattily attired bad guy Forrest Tucker made what bold claim?

Q306. Name a John Wayne film scored by John Williams and one by Henry Mancini.

Q307. "Termites!" This was John Wayne's explanation to a ground crewman about the bullet holes in his plane after an aerial dogfight with the enemy in what film?

Q308. In *The Desert Trail,* a 1935 Lone Star Western, what was Wayne's recurring action with chubby sidekick Edward (Eddy) Chandler?

Q309. Wayne asked James Stewart how long he had been practicing medicine in *The Shootist.* How many years did Stewart tell him he'd been a sawbones and how much did Wayne pay him for his services?

Q310. Just before the fadeout in *Dark Command,* Roy Rogers tells Texas-loving Wayne, "Ever hear what Shakespeare said? All's well that ends well." What was the Duke's comeback?

Q311. Wayne re-created his screen role in telescoped radio versions of what five films, and who were his radio costars?

Q312. What three actors who played John Wayne's fellow officers in Otto Preminger's *In Harm's Way* (1965) played church officials in the preceding Preminger movie?

Q313. In John Huston's *The Barbarian and the Geisha* (1958), John Wayne, as Consul General Townsend Harris, was sent to Japan by whom and what gift,

With Denny Meadows (later called Dennis Moore) in *The Dawn Rider* (1935)

among others, did he decide to present to the Shogun on their long-delayed meeting?

Q314. After moseying into town in the Lone Star Western *The Dawn Rider* (1935), Wayne stumbled upon some local mischief in which would-be tough Reed Howes had a stranger "dance" at the end of his six-gun. What was Duke's verbal exchange with Howes before brawling with him and ending up pals and rivals for the leading lady?

Q315. Wayne, of course, starred in Howard Hawks's *Rio Bravo* in 1959. This was the title originally to have been given to what earlier Wayne movie?

Q316. In what two movies did Wayne end up as a cripple?

Q317. Wayne generally wore a traditional ten-gallon hat in his hoss operas and bigger-budgeted Westerns but also donned a coonskin cap on in a number of his films. Name four.

Q318. Who "wrote" the onscreen prologue to Wayne's *Flying Tigers* (1942), his first World War II movie, and what was Wayne's status in the film?

Q319. What was Anthony Quinn's nationality in his two films with John Wayne?

Q320. Name the film from which this Wayne monologue came: "We can't turn back; we're blazin' a trail that started in England. Not even the storms of the sea could turn back the first settlers. And they carried it on further. They blazed it on through the wilderness of Kentucky. Famine, even hunger, not even massacres could stop them. Now we've picked up the trail again. And nothin' can stop us. Not even the snows of winter nor the peaks of the highest mountains. We're building a nation! But we've gotta suffer. No great trail was ever blazed without hardship. And you've gotta fight! That's life. And when you stop fightin' that's death. What are you gonna do, lie down and die? Not in a thousand years. You're goin' on with me!"

Q321. In how many pictures did John Wayne act? (This does not include documentaries, voice-over narrations for industrial films, or gag walk-ons, such as in *I Married a Woman* and *Cancel My Reservation*.)

Q322. What was Wayne's final line in *True Grit?*

Q323. British actress Anna Lee was Wayne's leading lady in *Flying Tigers* (1942). In what other of Duke's films did she appear in lesser roles?

Q324. Leigh Brackett was one of the rare female screenwriters who wrote action scripts (she was a favorite of Howard Hawks). Name at least four films she wrote for John Wayne.

Q325. In John Huston's *The Barbarian and the Geisha*, Wayne, as the towering Townsend Harris, had a hu-

With pre-Colonials Forrest Dillon and Claire Trevor

morous scene bopping his forehead and banging his head on the low door frames that were de rigeur in Japanese houses, drawing giggles from a gaggle of spying youngsters. What was diminutive fellow American Sam Jaffe's suggestion?

Q326. After a run-in with the King George's men under George Sanders's command, what order did John Wayne give his band of rebels in *Allegheny Uprising* (1939)?

Q327. "I'll be damned if she didn't get the last word in again. W-e-l-l . . ." This was Wayne's last line in what latter-day film?

Q328. On what song did Lauren Bacall and John Wayne, erstwhile singing cowboy of the mid-thirties, harmonize in *The Shootist*?

Q329. When called on the carpet for an infraction with his ship hours after the Pearl Harbor bombing, what did commander Wayne tell his superior, Franchot Tone, in *In Harm's Way* (1965)?

Q330. In the 1935 Wayne hoss opera, *The Dawn Rider,* a wedding ring became central to the action. According to a newspaper ad, what was the cost of the ring?

Q331. At Wayne's 1946 marriage to Esperanza Bauer, which of his screen colleagues were best man and matron of honor?

Q332. In only one film did Wayne have an onscreen mother: Agnes Moorehead in *The Conqueror* (1956). What was unusual about the casting?

Q333. What six John Wayne movies did Dimitri Tiomkin score?

Q334. Name the film in which Wayne did yeoman's work stamping out a cholera epidemic.

Q335. In what film, based on a famed literary work, was Wayne involved as a shill in a boxing scam in Northwest logging country, and who played the same part in an earlier adaptation of the story?

Q336. "We're all human. But, unfortunately, at sea there's no chance for us to enjoy our humanity." To what leading lady did Wayne make this observation, parrying her seductive approach?

Q337. "Wayne Means Adventure!" was the catchline used to sell *Hatari!* (1962) at the box office. The publicity went on to note that it was made by veteran Howard Hawks "who directed some of Hollywood's finest outdoor adventures including *Red River* and *Mogambo*." What was wrong with that statement?

Q338. Name three Wayne films in which he was a rodeo rider.

Q339. "She's a woman, Jamuga. All woman!" was a campy Wayne line in what CinemaScope epic?

Q340. "There's eight or nine cans in our munition dump marked 'Nitro USA.' I think I can find a messenger boy to deliver them." Wayne told this to his superior in what movie?

Q341. To whom and in what picture did Wayne give shooting lessons with these instructions: "Balance it in your hand and don't jerk the trigger—squeeze."?

Q342. Ann Dvorak, one of the popular leading ladies of the thirties and forties, starred with John Wayne only once. In what film did she star with him, and what song did she sing in it?

Q343. John Wayne was a star tackle on the USC Trojan team while in college. He later made one Western with another college football star turned cowboy actor. Who was it and in what picture did they work together?

Q344. What rather unlikely music name scored Wayne's movie *El Dorado* (1967)?

Q345. What was significant about assorted passages of music in Wayne's *Operation Pacific* (1951)?

Q346. Name two pictures in which John Wayne was Ward Bond's superior officer and two in which their positions were switched.

Q347. In 1951 the popular recording group the Four Aces had a big hit with "A Garden in the Rain." This song was a revival of the theme of what John Wayne movie?

Q348. In *Reap the Wild Wind* (1942), what was the name of John Wayne's pet monkey and the name of foppish Ray Milland's "talking" lapdog?

Q349. On what wartime flag-waver did ultraconservative Wayne work with several craftsmen he found too left-wing for his tastes and who became victims of the Hollywood blacklist several years later?

Q350. Name four consecutive John Wayne movies—one contemporary action adventure tale, one pre-World War II "war" film, one sports picture, and one sea saga—that were directed by Universal's journeyman director Arthur Lubin.

Q351. Although the prolific Western writer Zane Grey's works were film staples during the first half of the twentieth century, John Wayne appeared in an adaptation of only one. Name it. Who played the Wayne role in the earlier silent version?

Q352. In what Wayne film did a noted stage-star and screen character-actor play someone named Humphrey Agnew? In which one did he play Teddy Roosevelt?

Q353. Name two films in which Wayne donned blackface, or as his character called it, "Alabama tan."

Q354. What's the secret phrase Wayne shared with Patricia Neal, playing his ex-wife, in *Operation Pacific*?

Q355. "It's the greatest picture I've ever seen. It will last forever, run forever." Who has been quoted with making this comment about John Wayne's *The Alamo*?

Q356. Who narrated the prologue to Cecil B. DeMille's *Reap the Wild Wind* and how did part of that narration differ from the film's title?

Q357. Where was American pilot John Wayne from in *Reunion in France* (1942) and what was his response when "French" seductress Joan Crawford asked him if he was shot down?

Q358. Who was Wayne's nominal *Back to Bataan* (1945) leading lady (by default as one of only two actresses in the film) and what was their only other movie together?

Q359. An early indication of John Wayne's well-known patriotism was evident in *Dark Command* in 1940. What was his reaction to George "Gabby" Hayes, his partner, when hearing a group of schoolchildren singing "My Country 'Tis of Thee"?

Q360. In *They Were Expendable* (1945), what was Wayne's reason for wanting to transfer from newly introduced PT boats to destroyers at the outset of World War II?

Q361. What was Wayne's final line in *Pittsburgh* (1942)? It was the third time he used it in the film.

Q362. Name a Wayne war movie that featured five other serial stars (six including Wayne himself).

Q363. What was John Wayne's opening scene in *Operation Pacific* (1951)?

Q364. Who was the narrator of Wayne's *Sands of Iwo Jima* (1949) and what type of billing did costar John Agar receive?

Q365. Before galloping onto the scene in *Angel and the Badman* (1947), what did Wayne's character do?

Q366. In Howard Hawks's *Red River* (1948), Wayne played a cattle baron. What was his role in George Sherman's *Red River Range* a decade earlier?

Q367. Who was the recipient of John Wayne's compliment that "You look beautiful when your eyes shine like that"?

Q368. John Wayne played war hero and movie screenwriter Frank "Spig" Wead in John Ford's *The Wings of Eagles* (1957). Wead and Wayne both were buddies of Ford. Who played the Ford-like character in the film?

Q369. To what does the title of *Donovan's Reef* (1963) refer?

Q370. What nickname did John Wayne use for Marlene Dietrich in *The Spoilers* (1942) and what was his response when seeing her all gussied up in lace?

Q371. At the end of *Seven Sinners* (1940), Wayne chose his navy career over Dietrich. Whom did she go off with?

Q372. What were Wayne's tender words of proposal to Gail Russell in *Angel and the Badman* (1947) although he never came flat out and popped the question?

In the first of his two films with Gail Russell

Q373. *Wake of the Red Witch* (1948) was narrated by whom and who narrated the film's two lengthy flashbacks?

Q374. *The High and the Mighty* marked the fourth screen teaming of John Wayne and Claire Trevor. What other former Wayne leading lady also costarred in that 1954 film?

Q375. Wayne, of course, dabbled in directing on occasion. Name seven of his costars over the years who also directed films.

Q376. Name John Wayne's leading ladies in his three thirties serials and which one made a return appearance opposite him in a later film.

Q377. Which *Gone With the Wind* actress earlier costarred with Wayne in three of his Republic Westerns and which *Gone With the Wind* actress was a later Wayne leading lady?

Q378. In *Back to Bataan,* Anthony Quinn was a Filipino guerrilla leader under John Wayne's command and "Ducky" Louie, a Filipino youngster, was a village youth who played a significant role in Wayne's mission. In what later film did Quinn and the boy act together again?

Q379. When Donna Reed asked John Wayne for a whirl on the dance floor during a quiet shoreside moment in *They Were Expendable* (1945), what was his response?

Q380. John Wayne had a tiny part in what 1930 picture that starred Dixie Lee, who would soon give up her career to become Mrs. Bing Crosby, and Arthur Lake, who later would find everlasting fame as Dagwood Bumstead in the "Blondie" series?

Q381. In the 1943 Wayne comedy *A Lady Takes a Chance,* Jean Arthur was a pert little lady from back East who decided to take a cross-country vacation tour by bus. How much did it cost her?

Q382. The Inferno, an exotic nightclub, plays a prominent part of what John Wayne movie, and where is it located?

Q383. Before making his deep sea dive at the climax of *Reap the Wild Wind* (1942), what did Wayne promise to Paulette Goddard?

Q384. John Wayne's sidekick in *Dark Command* was George "Gabby" Hayes, who went on to become sidekick to Roy Rogers in many forties Westerns. Hayes and Rogers share only one scene in this Raoul Walsh film. What are they doing?

Q385. John Wayne explained to Lana Turner in *The Sea Chase* (1955) why he never married using what words?

Q386. Name Wayne's best-selling 1973 RCA recording.

Q387. True or false: Sgt. Barry Sadler, who had his one and only record smash with his recording of "The Ballad of the Green Berets," sang the stirring march in the Wayne Vietnam War film.

Q388. In *Allegheny Uprising* (1939), what was the name of Wayne's group of pre-Revolutionary War freedom fighters and how did he discourage rambunctious costar Claire Trevor from joining them on raids against both the Indians and the British?

Q389. Two then up-and-coming performers supporting John Wayne in *Reap the Wild Wind* (and earlier Ray Milland in *Beau Geste*) went on to stardom, costarring in one movie and much later starring (separately) in a stage and screen musical. Name them.

Q390. Name eight films in which John Wayne piloted a plane.

Q391. Name five actors who worked with Wayne *after* winning Oscars.

Q392. In Wayne's *The Spoilers* (1942), to what did the title refer and who played the title role?

As "Horse Soldier" Col. John Marlowe in Ford's late-fifties film

Q393. Name the nightclub thrush turned the screen Western's most famous cowgirl, who cowrote several songs for Wayne's *Rio Grande* in 1950.

Q394. Name three not so subtle similarities between *Reap the Wild Wind* and *Wake of the Red Witch*.

Q395. Besides *Red River* (1948), in which Wayne worked with both Harry Carey and Harry Carey Jr., and the films in which he worked with his own sons Patrick or Ethan, what Duke movie had both father and son in support of the star?

Q396. What was Wayne's term for William Holden in *The Horse Soldiers* (1959) and why?

Q397. To whom, and in what picture, did John Wayne fend off marriage with the comment, "If I wanted to get hooked, I'd let you hook me—but I don't wanna get hooked"?

Q398. In *Wake of the Red Witch* (1948), brooding, quick-to-fury John Wayne played a seafarer named Ralls. What was his first name?

Q399. What was Wayne's nickname in *In Old California* (1942)?

Q400. How did *Allegheny Uprising* end?

Q401. Veteran director William A. Wellman worked with Wayne in the fifties on *Island in the Sky, The High and the Mighty,* and *Blood Alley.* Name two films they made together two decades earlier.

Q402. What was Wayne's occupation in *Hondo* (1953) and how did he make his first appearance in the film?

Q403. Young John Wayne was a collegian who defeated star George Bancroft as an aging boxer in *Lady and Gent* (1932). Name one other picture in which they later acted together.

Q404. Chill Wills won an Oscar nomination for his performance in Wayne's *The Alamo.* In what other pseudo-historical film did they act together?

Q405. John Ford, of course, directed John Wayne in *Three Godfathers,* but who directed him in *Three Texas Steers* (1939), *Three Musketeers* (1933), *Three Faces West* (1940), and *Three Girls Lost* (1931)?

Q406. "We're out in the middle of nowhere looking for nothing in the wrong season," was Wayne's humorous observation about the treasure hunt he's on in what fifties adventure?

Q407. John Wayne starred as a character named Rod Drew, a cowpoke on a mission to find a missing girl and a hidden mine, in *The Trail Beyond* (1934), an adaptation of James Oliver Curwood's 1908 novel *The Wolf Hunters: A Tale of Adventure in the Wilderness.* Who starred in the role in the 1926 silent version and in the 1949 remake?

Q408. Over his career, Wayne filmed in Seattle, London, Honolulu, Rome, Houston, Baton Rouge, and in other locales worldwide. True or false: he never went on location in New York City.

Q409. Victor McLaglen, as John Wayne's military aide and drinking buddy in *She Wore a Yellow Ribbon* (1949), had what phrase to describe his superior?

Q410. What was Wayne's character's job in *The Lawless Frontier* (1934), *Lawless Range* (1935), and *The Lawless Nineties* (1936)?

Q411. In *Seven Sinners* (1940), her first film with John Wayne, newly resurrected star Marlene Dietrich unabashedly explained her character (a stateless saloon singer working assorted South Seas ginmills) in what words at the movie's start?

Q412. *Ombre Rosse* and *La Charge Heroique* were the Italian and French titles, respectively, of what John Wayne classics?

Q413. Name two John Wayne costars from the same movie who had No. 1 song hits on the record charts.

Q414. To what leading lady did footloose John Wayne say "I've got a saddle that's older than you are" to discourage her romantic interest in him?

Q415. John Wayne had a small role in a 1933 film with what star who later directed him in a classic of sorts?

Q416. In what film did Wayne support one of the major cowboy stars of the thirties who later died heroically while rescuing victims of Boston's infamous Cocoanut Grove fire?

Q417. Wayne made *The Shootist* (1976) for producer Mike Frankovich. In what earlier picture was Frankovich's actress wife Wayne's leading lady?

Q418. In Wayne's Lone Star Western *Rainbow Valley* (1935), Duke was an undercover agent who met up with grizzled postal carrier George "Gabby" Hayes. What was the name "Gabby" had given to his old model T?

Q419. Wayne's only Singin' Sandy Western was *Riders of Destiny* (1933), the first of the Monogram Lone Stars. How did the studio advertise this new type of outdoor action picture that was to have been a Singin' Sandy series? And what was George (not yet "Gabby") Hayes's role in this one?

Q420. In the nearly consecutive early forties films *Lady From Louisiana* and *Lady for a Night,* who was Wayne's blackguard nemesis, better known for his starring roles on the Broadway musical stage?

Q421. Name the gambling club Wayne opened in *Lady for a Night* (1941) and the rundown plantation of which Joan Blondell became mistress.

Q422. Other than *The Alamo,* Wayne starred in a number of films set in Texas—specifically those with Texas in the title. Name three of them.

Q423. In *Circus World* (1964), what superstitious omens presaged the sinking in Barcelona Bay of the ship carrying showman Wayne's circus to Europe, and what was the film called in Great Britain?

Q424. In what Wayne Westerns did both he and his leading lady have sidekicks?

Q425. How much did John Wayne charge Rossano Brazzi to lead him into the desert for what would turn out to be a treasure hunt in *Legend of the Lost* (1957)?

His *Quiet Man* wedding portrait with Maureen O'Hara . . .

Q426. Who narrated Wayne's *The Quiet Man*?

Q427. Where did the nearly obligatory Wayne barroom brawl occur in *Lady From Louisiana* (1941)?

Q428. How did Wayne meet leading lady Constance Towers in *The Horse Soldiers* (1959)?

and a similar one a decade earlier with Martha Scott in *In Old Oklahoma*

Q429. How did Wayne begin his wedding night in *The Quiet Man* (1952)?

Q430. Aboard what ship does pearl diver John Wayne find work in *Adventure's End* (1937)?

Q431. Who were the seven sinners in Wayne's *Seven Sinners*?

Q432. In 1950, Wayne for the first time became number one in the box-office popularity poll of the *Motion Picture Herald*. Whom did he dethrone?

Q433. Name the only actor to costar with Wayne in each of the three films in John Ford's memorable cavalry trilogy.

Q434. Angie Dickinson, who was young-lady-with-a-past Feathers in *Rio Bravo,* was also in two other films with Wayne and one that he produced (but was not in). Name them.

Q435. With what traditional song did the Sons of the Pioneers (as the Regimental Singers) serenade John Wayne and Maureen O'Hara in *Rio Grande* (1950)?

Q436. At the beginning and the end of *Lady From Louisiana,* where was Wayne found?

Q437. Name a pair of Wayne films two decades apart in which his characters and his leading lady's characters coincidentally had the same last names.

Q438. What does Wayne ask impish Barry Fitzgerald in *The Quiet Man* after first laying his eyes on Maureen O'Hara, who is tending a flock of sheep?

Q439. In a place called Dodge City, Wayne intoned the signature line, "Out here due process is a bullet!" in what film?

Q440. What Wayne film ballyhooed "The Screen's Greatest Adventure Star and Hollywood's Most Beautiful Woman"?

Q441. The 1933 Wayne Mascot serial *The Three Musketeers,* an updated version of the Alexandre Dumas novel, was reedited into a feature film fifteen years later. What was its title?

Wayne and Loren—together for the only time

Q442. What was Wayne's only movie for the short-lived Poverty Row company called Showmen's Pictures and who was the leading lady?

Q443. In Wayne's only film based on a Zane Grey novel, who was the leading lady and who was the Duke's sidekick?

Q444. Aside from Sophia Loren, his *Legend of the Lost* costar, Wayne acted opposite what three continental sexpots of the era?

Q445. Wayne and his horse Duke got equal star billing in the 1932 Western *Ride Him, Cowboy* for Warner Bros.

With Ricky Nelson in the 1959 Howard Hawks Western

Based on Kenneth Perkins's 1923 novel, it was first filmed in 1926. What was the title and who starred?

Q446. In *Rio Bravo,* there were two references to the Alamo, the subject of which would be Wayne's subsequent movie. What were they?

Q447. As a young journeyman actor, Wayne took jobs where he could find them and he made five films for Columbia Pictures in 1931–32, although he had consistent run-ins with tyrannical mogul Harry Cohn. Name Duke's five pictures for Columbia and the films' (not necessarily Wayne's) leading ladies.

Q448. In *Rio Bravo,* when belted for a second time by boozing deputy Dean Martin, who quickly apologized, what was Sheriff John Wayne's response?

Q449. Name four of Wayne's fellow players from John Ford's *The Quiet Man* who also appeared in Ford's previous Oscar-winning movie.

Q450. How long did John Wayne and Jeffrey Hunter's search for Natalie Wood last in *The Searchers?*

Q451. Two of Wayne's costars in *Circus World* (1964) were Rita Hayworth and Richard Conte. What other film did the two do together?

Q452. Name a Wayne film in which he playfully slapped his leading lady on the behind, less playfully kicked her on the rear end, and even dragged her across a field by her hair.

Q453. Between June 1932 and June 1933, Wayne churned out thirteen movies for five different studios. Name the ones that were *not* Westerns.

Q454. What was the name of the Coast Guard ship of which Wayne was in temporary command in *Sea Spoilers* (1936) and under what title was the film shot?

Q455. "Feels kinda silly acting like an avenging angel all the time" was a Wayne line from what latter-day action film?

Q456. In what early film was John Wayne an architect and in what one was he a truck driver?

Q457. Two of Wayne's least seen films of the 1950s, *Island in the Sky* and *The High and the Mighty,* had several similarities. Name five.

Q458. In *Reap the Wild Wind,* Wayne had a scene or two with actress turned gossip columnist, Hedda Hopper, who as a journalist became virulently anti-Wayne because of his politics. In what Wayne film did her actor son William Hopper have a supporting role?

Q459. Shortly after Maureen O'Hara, as his estranged wife, turns up at his post in *Rio Grande,* Wayne made what two observations about her?

Q460. When asked "How does a man get to be a sheriff?" by Angie Dickinson in *Rio Bravo,* what was Wayne's retort?

Q461. Wayne was a submarine commander in *Operation Pacific* in 1951. What earlier movie also had him in a sub?

Q462. Name the boat on which Eastern greenhorn Wayne and cast head from San Francisco to Sacramento and from which he and sidekick Edgar Kennedy are heaved overboard in *In Old California.*

Q463. In what film did Wayne, filled with loathing against Indians, confront a chief and spit out the words (that would be an anathema to a politically correct future movie generation): "Ya speak pretty good American for a Comanche. Someone teach ya?"

Q464. Besides working with such ladies of the stage as Geraldine Page earlier and Katharine Hepburn later, he had as a leading lady (twice) what other notable Broadway actress?

Q465. What were the three films Wayne made for Howard Hughes?

Q466. In the 1934 Lone Star Western, *Blue Steel,* who played the notorious "Polka Dot Bandit," for whom saddle tramp John Wayne was mistaken by Sheriff Gabby Hayes?

Q467. Besides *Circus World,* Wayne's 1964 adventure, in what earlier film was the Duke involved in a circus atmosphere?

Q468. What film did Wayne make directly after *Sands of Iwo Jima*?

Q469. What totally uncharacteristic Wayne gesture—not seen in any other of the Duke's movies—occurred in *Rio Bravo*?

Q470. After being bushwacked and winging nasty varmint John Mitchum (Robert's brother) in *Chisum,* what did Wayne tell him, anxious to plug him?

Q471. Noted author Ben Hecht and veteran director Nicholas Ray were among the writers in the credits of what latter-day Wayne movie?

Q472. John Wayne played an American general in what sixties film, the making of which inspired a literary bestseller by its writer-director?

Q473. When approached in a pool room and recruited by elderly priest Charles Coburn for his small college in *Trouble Along the Way* (1953), what did has-been football coach Wayne tell him?

Q474. Although currently called *Arizona* and *The Refugee* on television and home video, what were the original screen titles of these John Wayne films?

Q475. Ward Bond worked with friend John Wayne in twenty-one pictures (and on television in *Wagon Train* and special *Rookie of the Year*). Name the first and the last.

Q476. In the Wayne film *Red River,* Harry Carey Jr. acted with his dad, Harry Carey Sr. In what Wayne film did he act with his mother?

Q477. "I'd like to see you do twenty-five flanges" was a kinky-sounding line Wayne told his leading lady in what perfectly respectable sixties adventure film?

Q478. One of the passengers in *The High and the Mighty* (not Claire Trevor or Laraine Day) had flown with Wayne before in an earlier film. Who was it?

Q479. What was the original title for *Wyoming Outlaw* (1939), the next-to-the-last Wayne Three Mesquiteers Western?

Q480. When Wayne was getting his start in films, George O'Brien was a cowboy star. Name two films in which Duke supported O'Brien, one in which he starred opposite O'Brien's wife, and two later Westerns in which O'Brien supported Wayne.

With Geraldine Page—his only one with her and his only one in 3-D

Q481. In what movie did Wayne make this perhaps back-
handed romantic speech: "You baked today. I can smell
fresh bread on you. Sometime today you cooked with
salt pork—smell that on you, too. You smell all over
like soap. Took a bath, and on top of that you smell all
over like a woman. I could find you in the dark—and
I'm only part Indian."

Q482. What bit of Wayne wisdom did comely Ann-Margret receive from him during their search for stolen gold in *The Train Robbers* (1973)?

Q483. In *The War Wagon* (1967), the Wayne Western, what was the war wagon?

Q484. Wayne's screen protégé James Arness was Matt Dillon in *Gunsmoke* on television. What actor who worked with Wayne had played Matt Dillon in *Gunsmoke* on radio?

Q485. In *Brannigan* (1975), Wayne twice surprised the bad guys with similar but unorthodox entrances and uttered the same phrase. What was it?

Q486. What were Wayne's opening and closing lines in *McQ* (1974), the first of his only two cop movies?

Q487. "Hey, you got nice legs, too—for a copper." These were Wayne's parting words to his leading lady in what movie?

Q488. What actor who made his debut as a teenager with the Duke in *The Cowboys* was the son of a noted screen veteran who played in several Wayne movies?

Q489. Name eleven Wayne pictures aside from *Rooster Cogburn* (1975) in which the film title was the name of Duke's character.

Q490. What was Wayne's reactive statement in *Hondo* (1953) on learning that the Apache chief he had come to admire had been killed?

Q491. What is the connection between the Wayne's *New Frontier* (1939) and *The War Wagon* (1967), and what is the connection between *The War Wagon* and *Lady From Louisiana* (1941)?

Q492. In *The High and the Mighty* (1954), what was John Wayne's nickname and how long had he been flying?

Q493. Wayne handed his leading lady his spare bottle of whiskey and instructed her: "Dump that out and fill it with water . . . shows you how serious the situation is" in what film?

Q494. In *Ride Him, Cowboy* (1932), Duke's first Western for Warner Bros., what kind of six-shooter did he carry?

Q495. "Saddle up!" was a frequent John Wayne order in which of his films?

Q496. In *Operation Pacific,* Wayne's submarine rendezvoused with another during a battle lull and exchanged what two movies?

Q497. What part did Wayne regular Harry Carey Jr. play in *Rio Bravo* (1959)?

Q498. What professional advice did tough Chicago cop Wayne give to Scotland Yard commander Richard Attenborough regarding the kidnappers they both were seeking in *Brannigan* (1975)?

Q499. Name four Wayne pictures in which the quintessential American did not play an American.

Q500. In 1988 the National Film Preservation Act was passed, providing for a Registry by the Library of Congress in which twenty-five films a year would be permanently recognized as American cultural treasures. What was the first John Wayne movie to be enshrined?

Q501. What were John Wayne's last words on the screen?

Ready to pull his gun for the last time

From young saddle tramp to
grizzled old-timer

John Wayne Trivia
Answers

A1. To Henry Fonda, his martinet superior in *Fort Apache* (1948), when faced with warring Indians.

A2. Twenty-two with Ford, plus three on television; thirteen with Republic journeyman R. N. Bradbury, father of cowboy star Bob Steele.

A3. *Pals of the Saddle, Overland Stage Raiders, Santa Fe Stampede, Red River Range, The Night Riders, Three Texas Steers, Wyoming Outlaw,* and *New Frontier,* all part of the Three Mesquiteers series (1938–39).

A4. Sam; Clancy; Dog.

A5. *Big Jim McLain* (1952), *Island in the Sky* (1953), *Hondo* (1953), and *The Sea Chase* (1955). Arness also starred in *Gun the Man Down* (1956), which Wayne's Batjac Productions produced.

A6. *Red River* (1988).

A7. Standing on the bridge of his ship he bellowed "Stand clear!" as two of his crew were engaged in fisticuffs.

A8. He was the boss of a military construction battalion; she was a war correspondent.

A9. He was a small-town lawyer looking into the mysterious killing of an old friend.

A10. He was a would-be rodeo rider whose horse tossed him into her lap (she was a bank clerk trying to take his picture).

A11. John Ford's *Salute* (1929), Edward Sedgwick's *Maker of Men* (1931), William A. Wellman's *College Coach* (1933), and Michael Curtiz's *Trouble Along the Way* (1953).

A12. Tay Garnett's *Seven Sinners* (1940).

A13. In Henry Hathaway's *The Shepherd of the Hills* (1941), he was a "young" moonshiner from the Ozarks out to avenge his mother's killing.

Hellfighter Duke pretending to be the real-life Red Adair

A14. (a) Andrew V. McLaglen's *Hellfighters* (1968); (b) Richard Wallace's *Tycoon* (1947); (c) Dick Powell's *The Conqueror* (1956); (d) Melville Shavelson's *Cast a Giant Shadow* (1966); (e) William A. Wellman's *Island in the Sky* (1953); (f) Wellman's *Blood Alley* (1955); and (g) Henry Hathaway's *Legend of the Lost* (1957).

A15. Randolph Scott, Victor McLaglen, and Ward Bond.

A16. John Farrow's *The Sea Chase* (1955).

A17. The plot of 1985's *Witness*, starring Harrison Ford, was almost identical to Wayne's 1947 *Angel and the Badman*.

A18. *A Lady Takes a Chance* (Jean Arthur), *Reunion in France* (Joan Crawford), *Seven Sinners*, *The Spoilers* and *Pittsburgh* (all with Marlene Dietrich), *Without Reservations* (with Claudette Colbert), *Lady for a Night* (Joan Blondell).

A19. Joan Crawford, Claire Trevor, Susan Hayward, Jennifer Jones (she was Phylis Isley when playing opposite him), Loretta Young, Donna Reed, Patricia Neal, Geraldine Page, Sophia Loren.

A20. Eugene O'Neill's *The Long Voyage Home* (1940), Jack London's *The Abysmal Brute* (as *Conflict*, 1936), Zane Grey's *Born to the West* (1937).

A21. John Ford's *They Were Expendable* (1945) had a screenplay by Lt. Cmdr. Frank "Spig" Wead, whom Wayne played in Ford's *The Wings of Eagles* (1957).

A22. He was in *Angel and the Badman*, *The Fighting Kentuckian* and *The Alamo*, but not in *Bullfighter and the Lady* (1951) or *China Doll* (1958).

A23. It had left the town of Tonto bound for Lordsburg when it was stopped by Wayne, who had escaped from jail and was bent on settling accounts with the killers of his father and brother, after his horse turned up lame.

A24. The man who wrote more Wayne films (ten) than any other screenwriter.

A25. Victor Young and Elmer Bernstein each scored eight, while Roy Webb did seven.

A26. False. In an unusual arrangement, he and James Stewart shared top billing (Stewart in ads, Wayne on billboards) on *The Man Who Shot Liberty Valance* (1962). Stewart was billed over him on screen.

A27. Patrick was in nine films with his father, Aissa was in three, and Michael was in one. Michael also was billed as "assistant to the producer" on *The Alamo* and produced or executive produced *McLintock!, Cast a Giant Shadow* (coproducer), *The Green Berets, Chisum, Big Jake, The Train Robbers, Cahill, United States Marshal, McQ,* and *Brannigan.*

A28. Gary Cooper. Wayne appeared in films with all the others.

A29. Bette Davis and John Wayne never did a film together.

A30. *Stagecoach* (John Ford), *The Quiet Man* (John Ford), *The High and the Mighty* (William A. Wellman).

A31. Thirty-three for Republic, twenty-seven for Warner Bros.

A32. Character actress Mae Marsh did seven films with Wayne. Maureen O'Hara made five with him, as did Anna Lee.

A33. He took a bullet from a sniper.

A34. In the pokey in Timbuktu, after he celebrated the Fourth of July too loudly.

A35. "I don't hold workin' for women."

A36. It celebrated Republic Pictures's tenth anniversary with Wayne now its top star. He had also starred in the studio's first release, *Westward Ho,* in 1935.

A37. *Stagecoach, Allegheny Uprising,* and *Dark Command.*

A38. There were two—William Clothier and Archie Stout— who each shot twenty-five.

A39. *New Frontier* (1935) and *New Frontier* (1939). Both were Republic Westerns. The latter was subsequently retitled *Frontier Horizon* for television and for video release.

A40. Thirty-six: *Ride Him, Cowboy* (1932), *The Big Stampede* (1932), *Haunted Gold* (1932), *The Telegraph Trail* (1933), *Somewhere in Sonora* (1933), *The Man From Monterey* (1933), *Sagebrush Trail* (1933), *Blue Steel* (1934), *The Man From Utah* (1934), *The Star Packer* (1934), *The Lawless Frontier* (1934), *Texas Terror* (1935), *Rainbow Valley* (1935), *The Desert Trail* (1935), *The Dawn Rider* (1935), *Paradise Canyon* (1935), *Westward Ho* (1935), *The New Frontier* (1935), *The Lawless Range* (1935), *The Oregon Trail* (1936), *The Lawless Nineties* (1936), *King of the Pecos* (1936), *The Lonely Trail* (1936), *Winds of the Wasteland* (1936), *Idol of the Crowds* (1937), *Three Faces West* (1940), *Lady From Louisiana* (1941), *Dakota* (1945), *Tycoon* (1947), *The Fighting Kentuckian* (1949), *Sands of Iwo Jima* (1949), *Rio Bravo* (1959), *The Horse Soldiers* (1959), *The Sons of Katie Elder* (1965), *The Undefeated* (1969), *Chisum* (1970).

A41. Kris Kristofferson.

A42. *Two Fisted Law* (1932), *Adventure's End* (1937), *A Lady Takes a Chance* (1943), *Flame of Barbary Coast* (1945), and *Operation Pacific* (1951).

A43. In the 1950 version, *South Sea Sinner,* Macdonald Carey took the part that Wayne had in the original.

A44. Genghis Khan in *The Conqueror,* Cmdr. Frank W. "Spig" Wead in *The Wings of Eagles,* Consul General

In publicity shots with sons Patrick . . .

Townsend Harris in *The Barbarian and the Geisha,* Col. David Crockett in *The Alamo,* Col. Benjamin Vandervoort in *The Longest Day,* Gen. William Tecumseh Sherman in *How the West Was Won,* and John Simpson Chisum in *Chisum.* (Wayne also appeared as himself in a cameo in *I Married a Woman.*)

and young John Ethan

A45. *Stagecoach, Fort Apache, Three Godfathers, She Wore a Yellow Ribbon, Rio Grande,* and *The Searchers.*

A46. This was a line to Jeffrey Hunter in *The Searchers* (1956).

A47. Jack Palance.

Wayne with Paul Fix and Robert Mitchum in *El Dorado* (1967)

A48. Longtime friend Paul Fix was in twenty-five movies with Wayne between *Three Girls Lost* (1931) and *Cahill, United States Marshal* (1973).

A49. Three. "Rookie of the Year" on *Screen Directors Playhouse* (Dec. 7, 1955), "The Colter Craven Story" (billed as Michael Morris) on *Wagon Train* (Nov. 23, 1960), and "Flashing Spikes" on *Alcoa Premiere* (Oct. 4, 1962). All were directed by John Ford.

A50. He was at the train station during a severe North Dakota dust storm that he passes off to her and her Viennese surgeon dad, Charles Coburn, as "very unusual weather."

A51. In *The Alamo* (1960), there were Sam Houston (Richard Boone), Jim Bowie (Richard Widmark), William Travis (Laurence Harvey), and of course Davy Crockett (Wayne).

A52. In *The Shepherd of the Hills* (1941), he slapped hillbilly gal Betty Field for saying something bad against his dead mother just after slapping his horse, Roddy, to get him out of the scene.

A53. William Farnum (1914), Milton Sills (1923), Gary Cooper (1930), and Jeff Chandler (1955). Farnum, in fact, had a small role in the Wayne version.

A54. *The Conqueror, The Greatest Story Ever Told,* and *Allegheny Uprising.*

A55. Wayne was a prop man on Ford's *Four Sons* (1928).

A56. The original star, Robert Mitchum, was fired by director William Wellman for a prank in which one of the crew found himself bobbing in San Francisco Bay and Jack Warner demanded that Wayne replace Mitchum with a star of equivalent stature. Bogart, whose wife Lauren Bacall was the film's leading lady, demanded too much money, and Gregory Peck, the only other person on Wayne's short list, was occupied elsewhere.

A57. Jubilee. Goddard was aboard the rescue ship that picks him up after his own vessel was driven onto the rocks during a hurricane.

A58. Ralph Taeger played Hondo Lane in the short-lived *Hondo* series in late 1967; nobody had the Wayne role in the 1974 series based on *The Cowboys* (Wayne's character died in the film).

A59. He worked with Sir Cedric Hardwicke in *Tycoon* (1947) and with Sir Richard Attenborough (later) in *Brannigan* (1975).

A60. Shiloh.

A61. Earl Holliman and Michael Anderson Jr. (the latter was thirty-five years younger than eldest brother Wayne—and had a British accent to boot!).

A62. His real-life son, John Ethan, named for the character Wayne played in *The Searchers*.

A63. *Norwood* (1970).

A64. Lt. Tom Wayne.

A65. "Truly this man was the son of God."

A66. Jeffrey Hunter, Wayne's costar in *The Searchers,* would go on to play Christ in *King of Kings*.

A67. "Fella who half raised me gave it to me. He found me somewhere along the big cattle trail. Folks had been bushwacked by Indians I guess. He was a big fella—a cattleman. Swung a wide loop in his younger days, I think. Wasn't too careful about whose calf he threw his rope at. Most of the old cattlemen were like that. He raised me."

A68. Alabama of 1818 was the site of the action and Wayne was a rifleman with the Second Kentucky Regiment. Oliver Hardy, in one of his two latter-day movies without Stan Laurel, was Wayne's chubby pal.

A69. To Lana: "You're beautiful when you're angry." To Susan: "Yer beautiful in yer wrath!" Wayne and Hayward previously did *Reap the Wild Wind* (1942) and *The Fighting Seabees* (1944).

A70. *True Grit, Big Jake, The Cowboys, The Train Robbers, Rooster Cogburn,* and *The Shootist*.

With Vera Ralston and Oliver Hardy

A71. False: He wore a mustache in only the last two, although you'd never know it from the ads for *Rio Grande* (which had him clean shaven).

A72. Tay Garnett's *Seven Sinners* (1940) with Dietrich was the first; Preminger's *In Harm's Way* (1965) was the last—although he subsequently played an American general in *Cast a Giant Shadow* (1966), set several years after World War II.

A73. Henry Hathaway's *Trail of the Lonesome Pine* (1936) did not have Wayne in the cast.

A74. He played a World War II naval officer; she played a navy nurse.

A75. "Let's go home, Debbie," as he picked up the confused and terrorized Natalie Wood following her Indian captivity.

A76. *Blood Alley* (1955) and *The Shootist* (1976).

A77. "How to be a Lady" was the book, "Memphis Belle," the riverboat.

A78. The Careys father and son were in Howard Hawks's *Red River*. Harry Sr. died shortly thereafter and Wayne's next film *Three Godfathers* (with Harry Jr.) was dedicated to him with the opening lines "The Bright Star of the Early Western Sky."

A79. *Reap the Wild Wind* and *Wake of the Red Witch*.

A80. *Idol of the Crowds* (1937).

A81. She was Tulsa-born Phylis Isley. Immediately after making the Wayne movie she costarred in the fifteen-part serial *Dick Tracy's G-Men,* then vanished for several years and reemerged as Jennifer Jones in *The Song of Bernadette*.

A82. John Wayne and Roy Rogers were in just one film together: *Dark Command* (1940).

A83. True. *John Wayne Adventure Comics* appeared between winter 1949 and late spring 1955. There were thirty-one issues.

A84. *Sea Spoilers* (1936) and *In Harm's Way* (1965).

A85. Wayne's movie *Wake of the Red Witch* (1948) involved a trading empire called Batjak. He apparently liked the name and adopted it, changing only the final letter.

A86. *Lady for a Night* (1941), the lady being Joan Blondell.

With Sammy McKim and the future Jennifer Jones

A87. Thunderfish.

A88. Fess Parker, George Montgomery (*Davy Crockett, Indian Scout,* 1950), Arthur Hunnicutt (*The Last Command,* 1955), James Griffith (*The First Texan,* 1956), Robert Barrat (*Man of Conquest,* 1939).

A89. Although it's commonly asserted that it was Glenn Strange, who played the Frankenstein Monster in *Abbott and Costello Meet Frankenstein* and later was Sam the Bartender in the *Gunsmoke* TV series, it was actually Jack Kirk who was Wayne's singing voice.

A90. *Brannigan* (1975). Wayne was a Chicago police lieutenant. The finale was shot at the deserted Beckton Gasworks on the banks of the Thames.

A91. Josephine Saenz (Panamanian), Esperanza "Chata" Bauer (Mexican), and Pilar Palette (Peruvian).

Starring in the first of his two cop movies of the 1970s

A92. His first name was Lon; the complete surname was never mentioned. It was shot on location primarily in Seattle. Eddie Albert played his police department superior.

A93. Katharine Hepburn in *Rooster Cogburn,* Paulette Goddard in *Reap the Wild Wind,* Jean Arthur in *A Lady Takes a Chance,* Ina Balin in *The Comancheros,* Ann Dvorak in *Flame of Barbary Coast,* Gail Russell in *Wake of the Red Witch,* Vera Ralston in *The Fighting Kentuckian.*

A94. Seventy-six Westerns; thirty-two in a modern setting.

A95. *Lady and Gent* (1932) received a nomination for Best Original Story (it lost to *The Champ*).

A96. *Jet Pilot.* (The leading lady had long since become Janet Leigh.)

A97. (1) *Hondo.* (2) *El Dorado.* (3) *The Horse Soldiers.*

A98. He delivered those lines to "wife" Nancy Olson in *Big Jim McLain* (1952).

A99. In *Fort Apache* (1948), the nominal leading lady was teenage Shirley Temple (playing Henry Fonda's daughter—at least she got equal above-the-title billing) who went on to a distinguished second career in middle age with ambassadorships from both Gerald Ford and George Bush. In *The Horse Soldiers* (1959), Constance Towers was the female lead—her husband was actor (and Rock Hudson clone) turned diplomat John Gavin, Ronald Reagan's ambassador to Mexico.

A100. *The Cowboys* (1972), which indicated on the ads—and nowhere else—that the title was *John Wayne & The Cowboys*, making it in effect the only movie in which Wayne's name was part of the title.

A101. *Lady for a Night* (1941).

A102. *In Old Oklahoma* (1943), retitled rather quickly *War of the Wildcats*—presumably to avoid confusing with Wayne's *In Old California* of the previous year, and *Rooster Cogburn* (1975), renamed *Rooster Cogburn and the Lady,* out of deference to superstar leading lady Katharine Hepburn.

A103. *True Grit* (1969).

A104. Gene Pitney—who had a hit record of it, despite the fact that it was eliminated before the film's release although it is promoted in the press kit for the movie.

A105. Richard Nixon proclaimed it his all-time favorite movie.

A106. *Red River, The High and the Mighty, Rio Bravo, The Alamo, Circus World,* and *The War Wagon.*

A107. *Stagecoach* (1939), *The Long Voyage Home* (1940), *The Quiet Man* (1952), *The Alamo* (1960), *The Longest Day* (1962), *How the West Was Won* (1962).

A108. Gary Cooper and Cary Grant!

A109. Most of the film indicated that James Stewart was the shooter, but it turned out to be Wayne. Lee Marvin played the villain.

As cattle baron and trail boss Wil Anderson leading his youthful charges in *The Cowboys*

A110. Directed by John Ford, Captain, U.S.N.R.

A111. Ricky Nelson in *Rio Bravo* (1959), Fabian in *North to Alaska* (1960), Frankie Avalon in *The Alamo* (1960), and Bobby Vinton in *Big Jake* (1971). Tommy Sands was one of the many stars in *The Longest Day* (1962) but he and Wayne had no scenes together.

A112. Twenty.

A113. *Stagecoach* (1939).

A114. *Tycoon* (1947).

A115. *The Sea Chase* (1955) with Lana Turner; it was directed by John Farrow, Mia's dad.

A116. *Brannigan* (1975), which depicted the star in tie, cardigan sweater, and checkered blazer offhandedly wiping up a British pub in a send-up of the old-time barroom brawl.

A117. Howard Hawks's *Rio Lobo* (1970) and George Sherman's *Big Jake* (1971), the last film for each.

A118. Meeting the men of the VMF-247 Wildcats on Oahu he announced: "When the command meets the commander for the first time, it's like a wedding. Nobody knows how it will turn out . . . whether it will be a happy golden anniversary or a divorce. We'll see."

A119. "I love you [they kiss]. I'm glad I didn't marry one of those burst-into-tears dames."

A120. The boat is Chuka San; the first mate is Bronx-accented Chinese "peasant" Mike Mazurki, onetime wrestler.

A121. He's in a Red Chinese jail, talking to the imaginary friend he calls "Baby."

A122. *Three Faces West* (1940), costarring Sigrid Gurie and directed by Bernard Vorhaus, neither of whom had memorable Hollywood careers.

A123. Ray Corrigan was Tucson, Max Terhune was Lullaby, Raymond Hatton was Rusty, and George Sherman was the director.

A124. U.S. Army colonel John Wayne to Filipino guerrilla leader Anthony Quinn in *Back to Bataan* (1945).

A125. Director John Ford engaged Osa Massen for the job, only to learn that she was Danish, leading him to reportedly comment, "Scandinavian is Scandinavian," and get on with the picture.

A126. Marguerite Churchill played opposite Wayne in *The Big Trail* (1930), and in his next movie, *Girls Demand Excitement* (1931), she was the best friend of leading lady Virginia Cherrill.

A127. Jack Holt was the star of *Maker of Men* (1931) in which Wayne had a supporting role and later himself had a supporting role in Wayne's *They Were Expendable* (1945). Wayne and Tim Holt both starred in *Stagecoach* (1939).

A128. Henry Hathaway's *Circus World* (1964).

A129. Glencairn. Ergenstrasse.

A130. He was a skywriting pilot for a traveling fair in the first; a pilot vowing to avenge his father's death in a train wreck in the second; a pilot out to help his legionnaire pals from the clutches of desert rebels in the third.

A131. Wayne worked with Jim Mitchum in *In Harm's Way* (1965) and with Chris Mitchum in *Rio Lobo* (1970) and *Big Jake* (1971).

A132. Nehemiah Persoff played the renegade chieftain; it was the swan song for veteran director Michael Curtiz—his only Wayne movie aside from *Trouble Along the Way* (1953); Stuart Whitman repeated his role opposite Richard Boone in *Rio Conchos* (1964), which used a strikingly similar plotline.

A133. False. In this version (it had been filmed previously in a 1928 version and later in 1963), it was Wayne's mentor and longtime friend Harry Carey who was the Shepherd.

Semper Fi with pre–James Arness protégé John Agar

A134. *Riders of Destiny* (1933), Wayne's first Monogram picture, began their association, which lasted until *Tall in the Saddle* (1944).

A135. In both *She Wore a Yellow Ribbon* (1949) and *Sands of Iwo Jima* (1949), Agar costarred with Wayne. He then fell on hard times in lesser and lesser roles before turning up in Wayne's *The Undefeated* (1969), *Chisum* (1970), and *Big Jake* (1971).

A136. Very early in his career, he was in *Words and Music* (1929), billed as Duke Morrison and working for the first time with lifelong pal Ward Bond, and then had a bit in *Cheer Up and Smile* (1930).

A137. Duke played in *College Coach* (1933) with Dick Powell, in *They Were Expendable* (1945) with Robert Montgomery, and in *El Dorado* (1967) with Robert Mitchum, all of whom played Marlowe on the screen; in *Brannigan* (1975) with Ralph Meeker, the second screen Hammer; and in *The Conqueror* (1956) with William Conrad, television's Nero Wolfe.

A138. Bruce Dern.

A139. He mentioned to her that he was William Hickok of Abilene, Kansas, the onetime marshal, and subsequently told her, when she scolded him for abusing her hospitality, "Mrs. Rogers, you have a fine color when you're on the scrap."

A140. *The Spoilers* and *Pittsburgh* (both 1942), opposite Marlene Dietrich and Randolph Scott. (Actually the billing was alphabetical.)

A141. Forrest Tucker. Bruce Cabot. Victor McLaglen. Forrest Tucker. Sophia Loren (she gives him a haymaker).

A142. The setting was Arkansas (although it was filmed in the mountains of Oregon!); cantankerous Rooster was accused by the judge, who gave him the job, of killing sixty-four suspects in eight years; and he wore the marshal's badge for "two lustrums" (or ten years).

A143. John Ford's *The Horse Soldiers* (1959), which was Ford's only full-length feature set during the Civil War. William Holden was Wayne's costar.

A144. "A gun. This may be a trick. If it is, someone is going to get hurt," he tells his imaginary friend, Baby, before donning a smuggled Russian uniform and merely sauntering into the countryside unchallenged!

A145. John Ireland in *Red River* (1948).

A146. "Here Is Tomorrow." The film originally was called *Thanks God, I'll Take It From Here,* the title of the source novel.

Taking a hard right from Sophia

A147. Warren Oates.

A148. He tells this to real-life son Patrick Wayne as the arrogant twentysomething screen son he hasn't seen in "nine years and four months" after being smart-mouthed and yanking him off his horse into the mud and giving him a whuppin'.

A149. Twenty-three.

A150. Gotcha. Trick question. He never made a Korean War movie in uniform. *Big Jim McLain* comes closest, being set generally during that period, but he was a civilian in that one.

A151. Wayne to Robert Ryan, his second in command-turned-successor, at the end of *Flying Leathernecks* (1951).

A152. It fell to her to present him with his Oscar as Best Actor for *True Grit*.

Babs and the Duke with Oscar giving an ever-so-slight smirk

A153. *How the West Was Won* (three-camera process) and *Circus World* (single-camera process), in 1962 and 1964 respectively.

A154. *The Longest Day* and *The Man Who Shot Liberty Valance* (both 1962).

A155. The other forty-one stars were listed alphabetically, while Wayne took last billing—out of alphabetical order. He really should have been next to last, but instead he followed Stuart Whitman.

A156. *The Man From Colorado* was not a Wayne movie; it starred Glenn Ford and William Holden.

A157. Pedro Armendariz, in *Fort Apache, Three Godfathers,* and *The Conqueror*. His son, Pedro Armendariz Jr., later acted with Wayne in *The Undefeated* and *Chisum*.

A158. Luther Adler; Gig Young.

A159. Lana Wood, Natalie's younger sister.

A160. *Hatari!* (1962).

A161. *The Undefeated* (1969). Rock Hudson was Wayne's protagonist and Andrew V. McLaglen was the director.

A162. Gabriel.

A163. Wayne had left America because he killed a boxer in the ring and was returning to his ancestral home in Innisfree.

A164. Football stars Merlin Olsen and Roman Gabriel (Los Angeles Rams) in *The Undefeated;* tennis great Althea Gibson in *The Horse Soldiers;* wrestler Mike Mazurki in *Dakota, Blood Alley, Donovan's Reef,* and *Man in the Vault*, a Batjac production; baseball star Chuck Connors (Brooklyn Dodgers, 1949; Chicago Cubs, 1951) in *Trouble Along the Way;* football star Woody Strode in

The Man Who Shot Liberty Valance; Los Angeles Rams and Pittsburgh Steelers lineman (and onetime screen Tarzan) Mike Henry in *Rio Lobo*; Fortune Gordein, footballer and world's champion discus thrower, in *North to Alaska*; boxer Victor McLaglen, various films; heavyweight boxer Arthur DeKuh, *The Life of Jimmy Dolan* and *Baby Face*; wrestler Nat Pendleton in *College Coach*; wrestler Wee Willie Davis in *Reap the Wild Wind.*

A165. Fitzgerald was in both *The Long Voyage Home* and *The Quiet Man.* Shields also was in *The Long Voyage Home* and *The Quiet Man,* plus *She Wore a Yellow Ribbon.*

A166. In *The Man From Utah* (1934), his costar was Polly Ann Young. Their brother-in-law Ricardo Montalban worked with Wayne in *The Train Robbers* four decades later.

A167. He was a civilian pilot for the Army Transport Command. Lloyd Nolan was his pal in this one and in *Circus World* in 1964.

A168. Ward Bond was in twenty-one (and they worked together briefly on TV in "The Colter Craven Story" on Bond's *Wagon Train* and in "Rookie of the Year" on *Screen Directors Playhouse*); McLaglen was in four and Wayne had bit parts in his early days in two in which McLaglen starred. Andrew McLaglen directed five, beginning with *McLintock!* in addition to two non–Wayne-starring Batjac productions, *Gun the Man Down* starring James Arness and *Man in the Vault* starring William Campbell (both 1956).

A169. *In Harm's Way, Cast a Giant Shadow,* and *The War Wagon.*

A170. George Washington McLintock; Reuben J. Cogburn.

A171. (1) Lieutenant; (2) Captain; (3) Sergeant; (4) Captain; (5) Lieutenant Colonel; (6) Major; (7) Major; (8)

In Ford's *She Wore a Yellow Ribbon*

Colonel; (9) Lieutenant Colonel; (10) Captain; (11) General; (12) Colonel; (13) Colonel; (14) Lieutenant Commander; (15) Commander; (16) Colonel; (17) General.

A172. Sammy and Janet.

A173. Robert Marmaduke Sangster Hightower. He robbed banks.

A174. (1) Shirley Temple; (2) Adele Mara; (3) Frances Dee; (4) Ona Munson; (5) Mildred Natwick; (6) Jennifer O'Neill; (7) Elizabeth Allen.

A175. "To Captain Brittles—from C Troop. Lest we forget."

A176. Hugh O'Brian *(The Life and Legend of Wyatt Earp)*, Richard Boone *(Have Gun, Will Travel)*, Harry Morgan *(Hec Ramsey,* with Boone), and, of course, Ron Howard *(Happy Days)*.

A177. Bruce Cabot, who died shortly before production began. Cabot was in eleven Wayne movies from *Angel and the Badman* (1947) to *Big Jake* (1971).

A178. *Fort Apache, The Longest Day,* and *In Harm's Way.*

A179. Both Leroy Holmes (with Richard Hayman on harmonica) and Victor Young.

A180. "Never go to bed without making a profit."

A181. According to her tombstone, she was Mary Cutting Brittles and died eleven years before the film's action takes place.

A182. Hatari is Swahili for danger.

A183. In Rome in summer 1965.

A184. *Tall in the Saddle* (1944).

A185. *A Man Betrayed*, aka *Wheel of Fortune* (1941).

A186. He wrote the title song.

A187. In consecutive movies, Wayne did his macho if rather sexist thing with Elizabeth Allen in John Ford's *Donovan's Reef* and Maureen O'Hara in Andrew McLaglen's *McLintock!* (both 1963).

A188. He directed it to Sophia Loren in *Legend of the Lost* (1957).

A189. Later B-movie director Hugo Haas was Vera's papa in both *Dakota* (1945) and *The Fighting Kentuckian* (1949).

A190. *Dark Command* (1940).

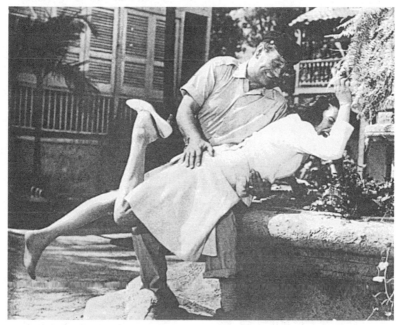

Not NOW! Politically incorrect—and defiantly so—with leading ladies Elizabeth Allen . . .

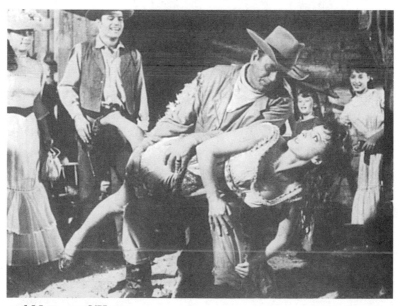

and Maureen O'Hara

A191. A CinemaScope jungle adventure called *Tigero* for Darryl F. Zanuck, the details of which are the source of the 1994 Jim Jarmusch–Sam Fuller picture, *Tigero—A Film That Was Never Made.* Wayne was scheduled to have a title role, a spear-wielding jaguar hunter.

A192. Ford was to have starred in *Hondo* and Tracy in *The High and the Mighty.*

A193. Wayne admonished the boys, "Don't rob banks." He was wounded by taking a knife just above the heart by a gang member.

A194. Trooper Thorn.

A195. At the barrel of the gun she is holding on him trying to get back the money Wayne took from her brother at a poker game.

A196. "Custer is dead." George Custer died at the Battle of Little Big Horn on June 25, 1876, but Wayne's wall calendar, which he is constantly crossing out counting down to his retirement, indicates the time is the week of March 6, 1876.

A197. *Rio Lobo* (1970).

A198. Elsa Martinelli, who joined his crew as a photographer.

A199. Just one—Pedro Armendariz, because he needed someone to translate. Wayne's greeting: "Buenos tardes, Jefe." Why Cochise spoke only Spanish is never explained.

A200. The exchange was from *Trouble Along the Way* (1953) between Wayne and Charles Coburn. They previously had done *Three Faces West* (1940).

A201. In *Big Jake* (1971), he'd tantalized bad guy Richard Boone with the million-dollar ransom money.

A202. Columbia Pictures and Walt Disney.

With Mitchum and old geezer Arthur Hunnicutt

A203. *The Spoilers* (1942), *North to Alaska* (1960), and *McLintock!* (1963).

A204. He was departing after forty years and was planning to push west to California until, as he was riding into the sunset, he was overtaken by Ben Johnson with news of a new appointment—as Chief of Scouts with the rank of lieutenant colonel.

A205. In *El Dorado* (1967), Wayne's hired gun told old friend Robert Mitchum's permanently hungover sheriff.

A206. A promotional tabloid herald published by Warner Bros. featuring illustrated stories on *The Cowboys, The Train Robbers,* and *Cahill, United States Marshal* as part of its fiftieth anniversary celebration in 1972–73.

A207. Rocklin. It was never indicated whether that was his first or last name.

Playing the whiskey-guzzling marshal in *True Grit*

A208. Strother Martin. In *True Grit* he was a wily horse trader; in *Rooster Cogburn,* a crotchety, Gabby Hayes–like river rat.

A209. Johnson was Trooper Tyree and McLaglen was Sergeant Quincannon.

A210. *The Quiet Man* came to Broadway in May 1961 as *Donnybrook!* with pop singer Art Lund in the lead.

A211. *The Life of Jimmy Dolan* (1933).

A212. In *The Comancheros,* he said this to costar Stuart Whitman, who plays a debonair gambler with a ruffled silk shirt. ("Monsoor" apparently was a Wayne-ism for "monsieur.")

A213. *The Lawless Frontier* (1934).

A214. *Tycoon* (1947). Laraine Day was the object of his (almost) affection.

A215. He was going from Poker City to Rattlesnake Gulch.

A216. *Three Godfathers* (1948).

A217. *The Comancheros, The Man Who Shot Liberty Valance,* and *Donovan's Reef.*

A218. *Angel and the Badman* (1947).

A219. Wayne tried to put a positive spin to reporters on the military debacle involving commanding officer Henry Fonda and his regiment at the end of *Fort Apache* (1948).

A220. In *The Man Who Shot Liberty Valance,* Wayne tells James Stewart, "I hate tricks, pilgrim, but that's what you're up against with Valance." In *McLintock!,* he says to troublemaker Leo Gordon before hauling off and decking him, "I haven't lost my temper in forty years, but, pilgrim, I'll make an exception . . . like hell I won't!"

A221. Moseying along tall in the saddle on his white pinto, strumming a guitar and singing "A Cowboy's Song."

A222. "A glass of milk. Plain. No rum. And no comments."

A223. "John Wayne—American."

A224. On January 22, 1901, the day that Queen Victoria died, according to the headline of the local paper. He was there to see the local sawbones, played by James Stewart.

A225. They went at one another in a coal mine in *Pittsburgh* and in saloon owner Marlene Dietrich's place and on the muddy street in *The Spoilers*.

A226. He commanded the First Illinois Cavalry unit and "Prior to all this insanity, I was a railroad engineer." He quickly qualified the statement by noting that he was an engineer in the construction of railroads.

A227. In the film, an offbeat "haunted house" cowboy movie, Wayne had a black sidekick, played by Blue Washington in the now demeaning but then fashionable stereotypically superstitious Willie Best style; the climactic fight was in a gondola swinging over an abyss and Wayne's character had it out with the bad guy's chief henchman. Ken Maynard starred in the 1928 version, in which Blue Washington had the same role.

A228. "Baby sister, I was born game—and I intend to go out that way."

A229. *Reunion in France* (1942), *They Were Expendable* (1945), *Three Godfathers* (1948), *The Wings of Eagles* (1957), and *How the West Was Won* (1962). All but the first were for John Ford. He also was seen fleetingly in the 1926 *Brown of Harvard,* his first screen appearance.

A230. In Winterset, Iowa, at 224 South Second Street.

A231. In *Girls Demand Excitement* (1931), a battle-of-the-sexes comedy, he was a psychology major and BMOC working his way through Bradford College as a gardener with no time for girls.

A232. *In Old Oklahoma* (1943).

A233. *North to Alaska* (1960), which at least four writers concocted from a play called *The Birthday Gift,* apparently unproduced in America.

With Kim Darby in *True Grit*

A234. Betty Field swung a sack of flour to Bond's head and managed to get Wayne square in the jaw instead, knocking him down.

A235. *The Alamo, Big Jake,* and *The Shootist.*

A236. This was his "I love you" speech to Katharine Hepburn at the end of *Rooster Cogburn.*

A237. Gen. Sterling Price, Rooster's beer-guzzling cat.

A238. *Big Jim McLain* (1952), which dealt basically with mopping up a Communist spy ring in Hawaii.

A239. Pomfritt, Connecticut.

A240. *McLintock!* (1963).

A241. (1) *McLintock!;* (2) *The Man Who Shot Liberty Valance;* (3) *Flame of Barbary Coast;* (4) *A Lady Takes a Chance;* (5) *In Old Oklahoma;* (6) *Pittsburgh;* (7) *True Grit;* (8) *The Fighting Seabees.*

A242. "The Girl I Loved Long Ago."

A243. As Rooster said, "Lost it in the war with Bill Anderson and Colonel Quantrill." In the earlier film he said that "It was in the war . . . the Lone Jack. Little scrap outside of Kansas City."

A244. "I'd like to help ya, but it's not my picture."

Duke and Kate in their only film together

A245. A truck driver involved in a race to deliver aviation parts to a waiting ship on the West Coast.

A246. The movie was *The High and the Mighty*. It was Wayne's first movie in CinemaScope; it had him cast, despite prominent top billing, in a sort of secondary role (as copilot of the plane, taking orders from younger Robert Stack, but managing to slap some sense into him at the climax); and it had Oscar nominations going to both of his leading ladies, Claire Trevor and Jan Sterling.

A247. Donlevy in *Allegheny Uprising* (1939); Carradine in *Reunion in France* (1942).

A248. With Tim McCoy, *Texas Cyclone* and *Two-Fisted Law* (both 1932); with Buck Jones, *Range Feud* (1931).

A249. *Stagecoach, Reap the Wild Wind, The Wings of Eagles, True Grit,* and *The Cowboys.*

A250. He shouted these words after hopping into his bulldozer and shoving a Japanese tank over a cliff in *The Fighting Seabees* (1944).

A251. It was the name of the camp near Da Nang in Vietnam under Wayne's command in *The Green Berets* (1968).

A252. "I won't be wronged, I won't be insulted, and I won't be laid hands on. I don't do these things to other people and I require the same from them."

A253. She was his niece in *The Searchers,* his fiancée in *The Man Who Shot Liberty Valance* (the one he lost to James Stewart at the end), and his wife in *The Green Berets* and *Hellfighters*. Although her part in *The Green Berets* ended up on the cutting room floor, her photograph survived for the Duke to gaze at. She also played Patrick Wayne's mom and Ward Bond's wife in John Ford's half-hour TV drama *Rookie of the Year* in which John Wayne turned up briefly as a reporter.

Ready to do battle with a rubber DeMillian squid

A254. One hundred dollars ("My children's rate").

A255. "Been tryin' to figure out what I liked about you. Come to find out that it's the easy style you unload a full-up wagon."

A256. (1) *Big Jim McLain*, (2) *The Quiet Man*, (3) *Legend of the Lost*, (4) *Jet Pilot*, (5) *The Wings of Eagles*.

A257. DeMille's *Reap the Wild Wind* (1942) had Ray Milland and Paulette Goddard billed first and third originally with Wayne and Susan Hayward second and sixth. Forties stars Milland and Goddard had passed their prime and were relegated to lesser billing after Wayne and Hayward when the film went back into theaters in the fifties.

A258. *In Old California* (1942) and *In Old Oklahoma* (1943).

A259. "Wrong, Mr. Pepper, 'cause no matter where people go, sooner or later there's the law, and sooner or later they find out that God's already been there."

A260. *The Alamo, The Comancheros,* and *McLintock!.*

A261. It was ten years and "I feel homesick for farm and see my people again."

A262. The U.S. Air Force.

A263. William Conrad did the narration, Merle Haggard did the singing, and the picture opened and closed with the identical shot of John Wayne on his mount surveying his spread, although both events took place weeks if not months apart.

A264. *Rio Grande* for Republic Pictures, *Rio Bravo* for Warner Bros., *Rio Lobo* for National General Pictures. Wayne was not in *Rio Conchos*.

A265. "Put out of your mind any romantic ideas that it's a way of glory. It's a life of suffering and hardship, an uncompromising devotion to your oath and your duty."

A266. She was a Probation Bureau officer looking into the welfare of recently divorced Wayne's young daughter. How the Probation Bureau got involved remains a mystery.

A267. Gail Russell in *Angel and the Badman* and *Wake of the Red Witch;* Vera Ralston (the boss's later wife) in *Dakota* and *The Fighting Kentuckian.*

A268. Ryan took orders from Wayne in *Flying Leathernecks* and gave him orders in *The Longest Day.*

A269. *Texas Cyclone* (1932), *Two-Fisted Law* (1932), *Dakota* (1945), *Red River* (1948), *Rio Bravo* (1959). (They also were in *How the West Was Won,* but in different segments.)

In Ford's piece of the stellar Cinerama Western

A270. *Ride Him, Cowboy,* made as the 1926 silent *The Unknown Cavalier* by Maynard; *The Big Stampede,* made as the 1927 silent *Land Beyond the Law* by Maynard;

and *Haunted Gold,* made as the 1928 silent *Phantom City* by Maynard.

A271. Thomas Mitchell.

A272. "Harbor Lights," a No. 1 pop hit in 1950 for Sammy Kaye. It also was a Top 10 hit for Bing Crosby and for Guy Lombardo.

A273. In *North to Alaska* (1960), Wayne's costars included pop idol Fabian and French actress Capucine. The action occurred in 1900 during the Alaska gold rush. In the film, Duke met Capucine at a Seattle dance hall/bordello called "The Hen House."

A274. Gen. William T. Sherman, portrayed by Wayne in his brief John Ford segment of *How the West Was Won* and in Ford's 1960 episode of TV's *Wagon Train.*

A275. Constance Towers, who starred in the 1968 revival of *The King and I* as well as the 1977 one with Yul Brynner; Katharine Hepburn, who starred in *Coco;* Lauren Bacall, who starred in *Applause* and *Woman of the Year;* Elizabeth Allen (from *Donovan's Reef*), who starred in *Do I Hear a Waltz?* and Maureen O'Hara, who starred in the 1960 musical *Christine.*

A276. In *Sands of Iwo Jima* two decades before, Forrest Tucker was in Wayne's marine squad, along with John Agar and Richard Jaeckel, who also were in *Chisum.*

A277. "Hell, it's just another Western with different costumes."

A278. As the daughter of a French general who'd brought a number of exiles to settle in America, Ralston was impressed by Wayne's comment after meeting her "on the run," as it were: "You're uncommon gracious. I'd sure admire to meet you properly."

A279. *In Harm's Way* (1965).

A280. Henry Hathaway's *Legend of the Lost* (1957).

A281. Gaston Glass (French), Jorge Lewis (Spanish), Franco Corsaro (Italian), and Theo Shall (German).

A282. *Angel and the Badman* (1947), *The Fighting Kentuckian* (1949), and *Bullfighter and the Lady* (1951), in which Wayne did not appear.

A283. He expressed that view while ogling buxom Janet Leigh in *Jet Pilot* (1957).

A284. They had basically the same plot, with Duke playing a lawyer exposing a crooked politician and falling for the bad guy's daughter. The biggest difference was that *Lady From Louisiana* was a period piece set in old New Orleans.

A285. In Orange County, California; in Brooklyn, New York.

A286. Wayne's artist friend Olaf Wieghorst, who had a small role in the film as gunsmith Swede Larsen.

A287. *Operation Pacific, Trouble Along the Way,* and *The Searchers.*

A288. *Central Airport, Reap the Wild Wind, The Fighting Seabees, Wake of the Red Witch, Sands of Iwo Jima, The Alamo, The Cowboys,* and *The Shootist.* He died offscreen in *The Man Who Shot Liberty Valance.*

A289. *In Harm's Way.*

A290. Roscoe Lee Browne played the part in *The Cowboys* (1972). In the brief TV spinoff series, Moses Gunn had the role.

A291. This comes from a quiet scene in *The Alamo* just before all hell breaks loose at the finale.

A292. Howard Hawks's *Rio Bravo* (1959).

A293. Wayne and Robert Mitchum were each nicked in the right leg by bullets at different times in *El Dorado.*

A couple of old cripples in "The Big One With the Big Two!"

Mitchum, favoring his leg, hobbled around with a crutch under his right arm until the climactic shootout, when, having to use his right hand to fire his six-shooter, he switched his crutch to his left arm and pretended his left leg was bad. Later he switched back again when Wayne, having been hit in his right leg in the gunfight and patched up, reached for his crutch and put it under his left arm. Mitchum pointed out, "You've got it under the wrong arm," to which Wayne retorted: "Well, how would you know? First you've been using it under one arm and then the other." (Whether this exchange was written into the script or ad-libbed to cover the earlier mistake and save re-filming remains a question.) In any event, the final scene had the two of them jauntily hobbling down the main street of town each with a crutch under the wrong arm!

A294. "Katie Dwayne. Born Ohio, no date. Married Bass Elder, September 8, 1850, Clearwater, Texas." Bass Elder was shot in the back following a card game.

A295. *True Grit* (1969).

A296. "Mine was taller!"

A297. Alfred *(How the West Was Won);* Lionel *(North to Alaska);* Emil *(Big Jim McLain, Island in the Sky, Hondo).*

A298. He drove up to the Harvard gate in an army tank.

A299. "You let me worry about that, Green Beret. You're what this is all about."

A300. In Los Angeles in front of the Great Western Savings and Loan, the bank for which Wayne was spokesman in the 1970s. It was created by Harry Jackson, commissioned for the 1984 summer Olympics.

A301. The stone read "John Bernard Books/Born January 29, 1843/Died [blank space] 1901." He made his way to the saloon in a horse-drawn streetcar of the Carson City Traction Company.

A302. Bruce Cabot *(Big Jake);* Neville Brand *(Cahill, United States Marshal);* Howard Keel *(The War Wagon);* Michael Ansara *(The Comancheros)*; Edgar Buchanan *(McLintock!).*

A303. Ed Ames.

A304. *Three Faces West* (1940). He was the leader of dust bowl farmers on the eve of World War II.

A305. "Mr. Chisum is a man who respects the law. Around here I'm the man who owns it."

A306. Williams scored *The Cowboys* (1972); Mancini scored *Hatari!* (1962). Their albums of music from these films have become collector's items.

A307. *Flying Tigers* (1942).

A308. Wayne periodically stomped Chandler's foot and gave him a right to the belly.

A309. Twenty-nine years. Wayne gave him four bucks for two visits and another dollar for medicine.

A310. "Shakespeare, huh? He must have come from Texas, 'cause we've been sayin' that down there for years."

A311. *Pittsburgh* (Screen Guild Players) with Marlene Dietrich and Randolph Scott; *Stagecoach* (NBC Theatre) with Claire Trevor and Ward Bond; *She Wore a Yellow Ribbon* (Lux Radio Theatre) with Mala Powers and Mel Ferrer; *Fort Apache* (Screen Director's Playhouse) with Ward Bond; and *Red River* (Lux Radio Theatre) with Joanne Dru and Walter Brennan.

A312. Tom Tryon, Burgess Meredith, and Patrick O'Neal also costarred in *The Cardinal* the previous year.

A313. He was dispatched by President Franklin Pierce as America's first representative, and he chose a bottle of liquid refreshment that he referred to as "good old Sourmash Tanglefoot."

A314. Wayne chided him: "You must be the joker in the deck," to which Howes retorted, "Well one thing's certain—I ain't the queen." Wayne's comeback: "I'm not so sure. You're actin' like an old woman."

A315. John Ford's *Rio Grande* a decade earlier.

A316. *The Wings of Eagles* and *In Harm's Way* (in the latter he lost his leg in battle).

A317. *The Big Trail* (he was a trapper turned wagon train scout), *Allegheny Uprising, The Fighting Kentuckian,* and of course, *The Alamo,* where he played Davy Crockett.

A318. Generalissimo Chiang Kai-Shek was credited with the opening tribute. Wayne was a civilian volunteer pilot (as were all of his men) with the famed Flying Tigers helping the besieged Chinese from across the border in Burma on the eve of Pearl Harbor.

A319. In *Back to Bataan,* he was a Filipino guerrilla leader; in *Tycoon,* the Peruvian cousin of American Laraine Day (whose father was Britisher Cedric Hardwicke).

A320. This was Duke's big speech near the end of *The Big Trail,* after disposing of no-good varmint Tyrone Power (Sr.), the scummy wagon master, and assuming the job himself.

A321. He's credited with 162 movies.

A322. "Well, come see a fat ol' man sometime," he said to Kim Darby just before galloping off.

A323. *Seven Sinners, Fort Apache, The Horse Soldiers,* and *The Man Who Shot Liberty Valance.*

A324. *Rio Bravo, Hatari!, El Dorado,* and *Rio Lobo.*

A325 "I think, Mr. Harris, you'd better raise the doorways or cut off your legs."

A326. "Sew up this valley so tight even a cricket can't get in without our say so."

A327. He said this as Katharine Hepburn rode away at the end of *Rooster Cogburn.*

A328. Gilbert and Sullivan's "Tit Willow."

A329. "My mission was to intercept and engage an enemy of greatly superior strength, sir. I can only take that one way—that my group was expendable."

A330. $23.90.

A331. Ward Bond was best man and Olive Carey (wife of Harry Carey and one of the players later in *The Searchers* and *The Wings of Eagles*) was matron of honor.

A332. Wayne was only six months younger than Moorehead.

A333. *Red River, The High and the Mighty, Rio Bravo, The Alamo, Circus World, The War Wagon.*

A334. *The Barbarian and the Geisha* (1958).

A335. *Conflict* (1936), from Jack London's 1913 novel *The Abysmal Brute*—filmed once before under that title in 1924 with Reginald Denny in the lead.

A336. To Lana Turner, playing a German spy incongruously dressed in a tight, low-cut white dress on a German tramp steamer freighter at the outbreak of World War II in *The Sea Chase* (1955).

A337. Hawks did not direct *Mogambo*. His and Wayne's friend John Ford did.

A338. *The Man From Utah* (1934), *The Desert Trail* (1935), and *A Lady Takes a Chance* (1943).

A339. In *The Conqueror* (1956), he said this about Tartar princess Susan Hayward to his blood brother, played by Mexican actor Pedro Armendariz.

A340. *Flying Tigers.*

A341. To James Stewart in *The Man Who Shot Liberty Valance.*

A342. She had the title role in *Flame of Barbary Coast* (1945) as saloon singer Flaxen Tarry, performing the rightly forgotten ditty, "Love, Here Is My Heart."

A343. In *Born to the West* (1937) Wayne costarred with Johnny Mack Brown, who had been a halfback on the University of Alabama's football team in the twenties.

A344. Nelson Riddle.

A345. Composer Max Steiner recycled some of his Oscar-winning score to *Now, Voyager*. The familiar main theme,

Football heroes turned movie cowpokes Brown and Wayne court leading lady Marsha Hunt

for one, was converted to a fox-trot for the officers' club dance toward the beginning of the film.

A346. Wayne outranked Bond in *They Were Expendable* and *Fort Apache;* Bond outranked Wayne in *Operation Pacific* and *The Wings of Eagles.*

A347. It was used in various musical interpolations and was the romantic theme of *Pittsburgh.*

A348. The monkey was Bananas, the pooch Romulus.

A349. Among those on *Back to Bataan* (1945) were director Edward Dmytryk and screenwriter Ben Barzman.

A350. *California Straight Ahead, I Cover the War, Idol of the Crowds,* and *Adventure's End,* all 1937.

A351. *Born to the West* (1937), later known as *Hell Town.* Jack Holt starred in the 1926 version.

A352. Sidney Blackmer as one of the passengers in *The High and the Mighty* (1954). He played Roosevelt in *In Old Oklahoma* (1943).

A353. *Allegheny Uprising,* in which he and his men prepared for a night raid against the British, and *The Spoilers,* in which he and fellow gold miners disguised themselves for the robbery of a bank that had been cheating them.

A354. "The old zing"—as when they kiss on a couple of occasions in the course of the film.

A355. John Ford, who was said to have shown up to help Wayne as a director and was sent off to do some second-unit filming, which may or may not have been used.

A356. Cecil B. DeMille read the prologue (as he did to practically every one of his films) and in intoning his praise of the great sailing ships of an earlier day, he noted that "They reap the harvest of the Wild Wind." "Harvest" apparently disappeared at the final title.

A357. He came from Wilkes Barre, Pennsylvania. He told her, "My plane was. I couldn't figure a way to stay up without it so I came down, too."

A358. Veteran character actress Beulah Bondi was the rifle-toting American teacher in the besieged Filipino village, who earlier was Wayne's backwoods, bitter Aunt Mollie in *The Shepherd of the Hills* (1941).

A359. "Gives me goose pimples," Wayne admits. "Sick?" Gabby asks him. "No, just proud."

A360. "Can't build a navy reputation riding a plywood dream."

A361. He joshingly told costar Randolph Scott, his partner in the tale, "I love ya, Cash. So help me, Hannah, I love ya."

A362. *Flying Tigers* (1942) featured in its cast John Carroll (star of *Zorro Rides Again,*) Paul Kelly *(The Secret Code),* Tom Neal *(Jungle Girl),* Gordon Jones *(The Green Hornet),* and Richard Crane *(Mysterious Island).*

A363. He was emerging from the jungle on a Pacific Island carrying a baby and leading a bunch of kids and nuns to be evacuated on his submarine.

A364. Arthur Franz, who played one of the squad members, did the voice-over narration, and John Agar was in the film "by arrangement with David O. Selznick" for whom he, ironically, never made a movie but apparently was under contract.

A365. He was a deputy riding with Wyatt Earp in Tombstone.

A366. He was a rustler-fighting special deputy with Three Mesquiteer pals Ray Corrigan and Max Terhune.

A367. Vera Ralston in *The Fighting Kentuckian* (1949).

A368. Ward Bond.

A369. It is the bar owned by Wayne on the South Pacific island where he and pal Jack Warden decided to stay after the war.

A370. He kept referring to her as "Sport," and when she sashayed around him enticingly, he commented, "You'd look good to me, baby, in a burlap bag!"

A371. Curiously, Marlene Dietrich went off with one of the lesser players, Albert Dekker, at the fadeout.

A372. "Look, does a lot of fooferaw and nonsense have to go with it? I'm not gonna stand for a lot of dressin' up and a batch of jabberin' people lookin' at me just because I'm gettin' married."

A373. Costar Gig Young told the story à la *Moby Dick*'s Ishmael. Secondary leading lady Adele Mara narrated the first flashback and Luther Adler the second.

A374. Laraine Day.

A375. Robert Montgomery (from *They Were Expendable*). Frank Sinatra, Richard Widmark, Kirk Douglas, Richard Attenborough, Mel Ferrer, and Ron Howard. James Stewart also directed, but only on television.

A376. Dorothy Gulliver in *Shadow of the Eagle* (1932), Shirley Grey in *The Hurricane Express* (1932), and Ruth Hall in *The Three Musketeers* (1933). Hall subsequently costarred with him in *The Man From Monterey* (1933).

A377. Ann Rutherford, who played Scarlett O'Hara's sister, Careen, was Wayne's leading lady in *The Oregon Trail, The Lawless Nineties,* and *The Lonely Trail* (all 1936). Ona Munson, who portrayed Belle Watling, had the title role opposite Wayne in *Lady From Louisiana* (1941).

A378. In *Black Gold* (1947), they were American Indian father and adopted Chinese son.

A379. "Listen, sister, I don't dance. And I can't take time out to learn. All I wanna do is get out of here."

A380. *Cheer Up and Smile,* Duke's movie that preceded his star-making part in *The Big Trail.*

A381. It cost $137.50 for seventeen days, all expenses paid.

A382. It's a flashy joint in the town of Temple City in *A Man Betrayed* (1941).

A383. "I'll bring you rainbow fish for breakfast."

A384. Hayes, as a grizzled jack-of-all-trades dentist/surgeon/knife sharpener/barber, is giving uncharacteristically foppish Rogers a shave in his frontier emporium.

A385. "I like to run my own ship."

A386. "America, Why I Love Her."

A387. False. It was performed by a chorus under Dimitri Tiomkin's direction.

A388. The patriots were called The Black Boys, and after disguising themselves in Indian war paint, Wayne told them to strip to the waist.

A389. Susan Hayward and Robert Preston, who acted together in *Tulsa* (1949) and subsequently starred in *Mame* — she on the stage in 1968 in Las Vegas and he in the 1974 film version.

A390. *Central Airport* (1933), *Flying Tigers* (1942), *Flying Leathernecks* (1951), *Island in the Sky* (1953), *The High and the Mighty* (1954), *The Wings of Eagles* (1957), *Jet Pilot* (1950/1957). He was a downed pilot in *Reunion in France* (1942) but was not seen flying.

A391. Victor McLaglen, Thomas Mitchell, Barry Fitzgerald, George Kennedy, and James Stewart.

A392. "Spoilers" were those stealing gold illegally from mining claims — not claim-jumpers — and they were played by Randolph Scott, a crafty gold commissioner; Margaret Lindsay, Wayne's girlfriend; Samuel S. Hinds, her uncle, a crooked judge; and Charles Halton, an unscrupulous mining town lawyer.

A393. Dale Evans.

A394. John Wayne played a captain who intentionally scuttled his ship, had an encounter with a giant octopus, and died underwater on a diving mission.

A395. In *The Trail Beyond* (1934), both Noah Beery and Noah Beery Jr. had supporting roles.

A396. Duke referred to Holden, playing a military doctor, as "croaker," remembering with bitterness his wife's death from cancer a number of years before, unable to be saved by surgeons.

A397. He said this to costar Jean Arthur in *A Lady Takes a Chance* (1943).

A398. Like TV's Lieutenant Columbo he was given none, as in the exchange between Wayne and petty tyrant Luther Adler, who had fished him out of the ocean where he was adrift: "What's your name?" "Ralls." "Your full name." "*Captain* Ralls."

A399. Boston.

A400. John Wayne pledged Claire Trevor his love, then headed for the Tennessee hills with his men to pursue the revolution, prompting Trevor to ride after him "to be with my man."

A401. *Central Airport* and *College Coach* (both 1933).

A402. He was a dispatch rider and U.S. Cavalry scout and was first seen walking out of the desert, saddle over his shoulder, trailed by his dog.

A403. Bancroft played Sheriff Curly Wilcox in *Stagecoach*.

A404. Wills was one of Wayne's "Black Boys" in *Allegheny Uprising*.

A405. George Sherman, Armand Schaefer and Colbert Clark, Bernard Vorhaus, Sidney Lanfield.

A406. Henry Hathaway's *Legend of the Lost*.

A407. Robert McKim in 1926; Kirby Grant in 1949.

A408. True.

A409. "Captain Darlin'."

A410. In the first, he was a saddle tramp tracking a wanted outlaw to avenge his parents' killing; in the second, he was an undercover lawman investigating cattle rustling and mine claim jumping; in the third, he was an undercover government agent sent to find the men terrorizing homesteaders in Wyoming territory in the 1890s.

A411. "I make rough seas . . . I set the jungle on fire . . . I'm a *bad* influence."

A412. *Stagecoach* and *She Wore a Yellow Ribbon.*

A413. Dean Martin and Ricky Nelson, who were in *Rio Bravo* with the Duke. Dean's No. 1 hits included "That's Amore" and "Memories Are Made of This"; Ricky's included "Poor Little Fool" and "Travelin' Man." Walter Brennan, also from that movie, had several records on the charts, but he didn't make it to the top. Other Wayne costars who hit No. 1 as pop singers were Glen Campbell, Bobby Vinton, and Frankie Avalon. Fabian never had a No. 1 hit and Paul Anka, who did, technically never costarred with Wayne although both were in *The Longest Day.*

A414. Ann-Margret in *The Train Robbers* (1973).

A415. Dick Powell was the star-turned-director who worked with Wayne in *College Coach* (1933) and two decades later directed him in *The Conqueror* (1956).

A416. *Range Feud* (1931), starring Buck Jones. It was Wayne's first Western after *The Big Trail.*

A417. Binnie Barnes, Mrs. Mike Frankovich, costarred with the Duke in *In Old California.*

A418. "Nugget Nell."

A419. "John Wayne . . . He's a soft-singing, hard-fighting hombre!" Hayes was leading lady Cecilia Parker's pop, half owner of a gold mine that the bad guys want.

A420. Ray Middleton.

A421. The gambling emporium was "The King's Club" and the plantation "The Shadows."

A422. *Texas Cyclone* (1932), *Texas Terror* (1935), *Three Texas Steers* (1939).

A423. Wayne first had broken a mirror and then had placed his Stetson on a bed. In England the movie was retitled *The Magnificent Showman.*

A424. In *In Old California* (1942), Edgar Kennedy was the Duke's sidekick and Patsy Kelly was the sidekick of Binnie Barnes; in *Somewhere in Sonora* (1933), Duke has two sidekicks (Frank Rice and Billy Franey) and female lead Shirley Palmer has one (Ann Faye).

A425. He charged $4,000.

A426. Ward Bond, who played the village priest.

A427. In a ladies' dress shop with the Duke taking on half a dozen bad guys headed by dense Jack Pennick.

A428. He kicked down the door of her Mississippi mansion and strode in to introduce himself and his officers.

A429. He kicked down the door of his and Maureen O'Hara's bedroom after she locked him out in a pique because her dowry (350 pounds in gold) and possessions had been kept from her by her irate brother, played by Victor McLaglen.

A430. The whaling vessel *Mary Drew.*

A431. Nobody. The title referred to Café Seven Sinners, the joint where chanteuse Marlene Dietrich performed.

A432. Bing Crosby.

A433. Victor McLaglen played Sgt. Maj. Quincannon in both *She Wore a Yellow Ribbon* and *Rio Grande* and was also in *Fort Apache,* as a different character (Dick Foran played Quincannon in that one).

A434. Angie played Duke's wife in the imaginary film-within-a-film in *I Married a Woman* (1958) and was in *Cast a Giant Shadow* (but shared no scenes with him). She

As Col. Mike Kirby in his (and codirector Ray Kellogg's) Vietnam War paean

also costarred opposite James Arness in the Batjac production, *Gun the Man Down* (1956).

A435. "I'll take you home again, Kathleen."

A436. In a romantic shipboard clinch with leading lady Ona Munson.

A437. In *Hondo,* Wayne's last name was Lane and Geraldine Page played Mrs. Lowe; in *The Train Robbers,* Wayne's last name again was Lane and Ann-Margret was Mrs. Lowe.

A438. "Hey, is that real? She couldn't be."

A439. *The Green Berets* (1968), Dodge City being the name of one of the American troops' jungle camps in Vietnam's Mekong Delta.

A440. *Rio Grande,* that brought him together with Maureen O'Hara for the first time.

A441. *Desert Command.*

A442. *His Private Secretary* (1933). Evalyn Knapp had the title role.

A443. The movie was *Born to the West* (1937), the actress was Marsha Hunt, and the sidekick was Sid Saylor.

A444. Capucine in *North to Alaska* (1960), Claudia Cardinale in *Circus World* (1964), and Elsa Martinelli in *Hatari!* (1962).

A445. *The Unknown Cavalier,* starring Ken Maynard and his horse Tarzan.

A446. The only hotel in town was The Alamo and the song the Mexican band played in the local saloon was, as Ricky Nelson pointed out to Wayne, "De Guella," the "Cutthroat Song," which was played at the siege of the Alamo. "De Guella" was part of Dimitri Tiomkin's score in both films.

A447. *Men Are Like That* (aka *Arizona*) with Laura LaPlante (he played a West Point graduate); *Range Feud,* the Buck Jones Western with Susan Fleming; *Maker of Men* with Joan Marsh (Duke's a football player under coach Jack Holt); and two 1932 Tim McCoy cowboy flicks, *Texas Cyclone* (with Shirley Grey) and *Two-Fisted Law* (with Alice Day).

A448. "Sorry don't get it done, Dude. That's the second time you hit me. Don't ever do it again!"

A449. Maureen O'Hara, Barry Fitzgerald, Arthur Shields, and Mae Marsh all were in Ford's *How Green Was My Valley* a decade earlier.

A450. Five years.

A451. *They Came to Cordura* (1959).

A452. *The Quiet Man* (1952).

A453. *Lady and Gent, The Hurricane Express* (serial), *The Three Musketeers* (serial), *Central Airport, The Life of Jimmy Dolan, His Private Secretary,* and *Baby Face.*

A454. The ship was Niobe; the initial title, *Casey of the Coast Guard.* The title was changed, presumably, since nobody named Casey was in the film. Duke played one Bob Randall.

A455. *McQ* (1974).

A456. An architect in *Three Girls Lost* (1931); a truck driver in *California Straight Ahead* (1937).

A457. They both had Wayne as a pilot, William A. Wellman as director, an Ernest K. Gann novel as a source, Archie Stout as cinematographer, and character actors Ann Doran, Paul Fix, and Regis Toomey in supporting roles.

A458. *The High and the Mighty* (1954).

A459. "Number one—you're a fine figure of a woman. Number two—you probably haven't eaten yet."

A460. "Just lazy. Tired of selling his gun all over. Decides to sell it in one place."

A461. John Ford's *Men Without Women* two decades earlier.

A462. Mary Anne.

A463. *The Searchers* (1956).

A464. Colleen Dewhurst in both *The Cowboys* and *McQ.*

A465. *Jet Pilot, Flying Leathernecks,* and *The Conqueror.*

A466. Stuntman Yakima Canutt, Wayne's pal and frequent fight double, had the part.

A467. The 1939 Three Mesquiteers entry, *Three Texas Steers,* in which he and pals Ray Corrigan and Max Terhune ride to the rescue of circus owner Carole Landis.

A468. *Jet Pilot,* which did not see the light of day for another seven years.

A469. He kissed grizzled Walter Brennan (on the top of the head).

A470. "Draw! Please draw!"

A471. *Circus World,* in which Ben Hecht was one of the writers of the screenplay, based on a story concocted by Nicholas Ray with fellow director Philip Yordan.

A472. Comedy director Melville Shavelson's dramatic *Cast a Giant Shadow* (1966) inspired his humorous *How to Make a Jewish Movie.*

A473. "I've been kicked out of the Big Ten, the Ivy League, and the Southern Conference. They wouldn't even let me coach at Alcatraz."

A474. *Arizona* was *Men Are Like That* (1931) and *The Refugee* was *Three Faces West* (1940).

A475. *Words and Music* (1929) and *Rio Bravo* (1959).

A476. In *The Searchers,* Harry Carey Jr.'s real-life mother Olive Carey played his screen mom.

A477. He told this to trapeze hopeful Claudia Cardinale in *Circus World* (a flange being "carny"-speak for one-armed twists while hanging from the trapeze).

A478. Paul Kelly and the Duke were flying buddies over a decade earlier in *Flying Tigers.*

A479. *Wyoming Outlaw* (1939) was filmed under the title *Oklahoma Outlaws,* for reasons never explained, since it was set in Wyoming.

A480. Wayne had small roles in O'Brien's *Salute* (1929) and *A Rough Romance* (1930) and made his big movie splash opposite Marguerite Churchill (later Mrs. George O'Brien) in *The Big Trail* (1930). O'Brien had supporting roles in Wayne's *Fort Apache* and *She Wore a Yellow Ribbon* in the late forties.

A481. Duke said this to Geraldine Page in *Hondo*.

A482. "When I start plying a woman with whiskey, it's time to throw the key in the water bucket and ride on."

A483. An ironclad stagecoach topped with a gatling gun, used by land baron Bruce Cabot to periodically transfer his gold with a heavily armed entourage.

A484. William Conrad, one of Genghis Khan's horde in *The Conqueror* (1956).

A485. He kicked down the door and growled "Knock, knock."

A486. He was first heard (but not seen) saying "Hello . . . oh, nuts!" as his hand reached for the phone and picked up the receiver during an introductory scene hangover. He was last seen telling Eddie Albert (his superior in the movie), "There's a bar over there. Let's get a drink."

A487. He said this to Donna Reed, as a child welfare officer, as she walks away with his tomboy daughter Sherry Jackson at the end of *Trouble Along the Way* (1953).

A488. The then-youngster was Robert Carradine; his famous dad, John, acted with Wayne in *Stagecoach, Reunion in France, The Man Who Shot Liberty Valance,* and *The Shootist.*

A489. *Brannigan, McQ, McLintock!, Pittsburgh, Chisum, Big Jake, Big Jim McLain, Cahill, United States Marshal, Hondo, Randy Rides Alone,* and *Donovan's Reef.*

A490. "Everybody gets dead. It was his turn."

A491. In *New Frontier,* Wayne acted with Jennifer Jones (then Phylis Isley), while in *The War Wagon,* one of his costars was her son Robert Walker Jr. The connection between *The War Wagon* and *Lady From Louisiana* was that Wayne's costar Howard Keel (in the former) and Ray Middleton (in the latter) each starred in the Irving Berlin musical *Annie Get Your Gun,* Middleton in the original stage version and Keel in the movie.

A492. Wayne was called "Whistlin' Dan" (he was constantly whistling the film's title tune) and, as his character admitted, "I've been flyin' since 1917 and I don't like this sort of thing [impending ditching in the Pacific] any more than you do." Attempting to reassure the passengers, he went on, "Now comes the hard part. Think you can take it?"

A493. The Duke said this to Sophia Loren as the two of them find themselves stranded in the desert with empty cantoons in *Logend of tho Loot.*

A494. A .38 mounted on a .45 frame, which, as he noted "takes the kick out of it."

A495. *Sands of Iwo Jima.*

A496. The Duke's men swapped Jack Benny's *George Washington Slept Here* for Cary Grant's *Destination Tokyo.*

A497. Although his name is prominent in the opening credits, Carey is not in the film. His part was left on the cutting room floor.

A498. "If it was up to me, I'd get some men out thumping the streets, passing out some 'E Pluribus Unum.' That's what ninety percent of police work is today."

A499. *The Conqueror* (a Mongol warrior), *The Greatest Story Ever Told* (a Roman centurion), *The Sea Chase* (a German freighter captain), and *The Long Voyage Home* (a Swedish seaman).

A500. *The Searchers,* included among the initial twenty-five in 1989.

A501. In *The Shootist,* after bellying up to the bar in preparation for the climactic shoot-out, he announced to the saloonkeeper, "This is my birthday. Gimme the best [whiskey] in the house," and then, plunking down a dollar, added, "Thank you, sir."

With longtime pal and frequent fellow player Ward Bond in the mid-fifties John Ford masterpiece

Muddied pals John Wayne and Maureen O'Hara in *McLintock!*

More Citadel Entertainment Fun Facts and Interesting Trivia

Ask for any of these books at your bookstore. Or to order direct from the publisher, call 1-800-447-BOOK (MasterCard or Visa), or send a check or money order for the books purchased (plus $4.00 shipping and handling for the first book ordered and 75¢ for each additional book) to Carol Publishing Group, 120 Enterprise Avenue, Dept. 1660, Secaucus, NJ 07094.

The Critics Were Wrong: The Most Misguided Movie Reviews and Film Criticism Gone Wrong by Ardis Sillick & Michael McCormick $12.95 paper (#51722)

Film Flubs: Memorable Movie Mistakes by Bill Givens $7.95 paper (#51161)

Also Available:
   Son of Film Flubs by Bill Givens $7.95 paper (#51279)

   Film Flubs: The Sequel by Bill Givens $7.95 paper (#51360)

Final Curtain: Deaths of Noted Movie and TV Personalities by Everett G. Jarvis $17.95 paper (#51646)

The "Seinfeld" Aptitude Test by Beth B. Golub $8.95 paper (#51583)

701 Toughest Movie Trivia Questions of All Time by William MacAdams and Paul Nelson $9.95 paper (#51700)

Starfleet Academy Entrance Exam by Peggy Robin $9.95 paper (#51695)

The TV Theme Song Trivia Book by Vincent Terrace $9.95 paper (#51786)

1,201 Toughest TV Trivia Questions of All Time by Vincent Terrace $9.95 paper (#51730)

The Ultimate Clint Eastwood Trivia Book by Lee Pfeiffer & Michael Lewis $8.95 paper (#51789)

The Ultimate James Bond Trivia Book by Michael Lewis $8.95 paper (#51793)

The Ultimate John Wayne Trivia Book by Alvin H. Marill $9.95 paper (#51660)

What's Your "Cheers" I.Q.? by Mark Wenger $9.95 paper (#51780)

What's Your "Friends" I.Q.? by Stephen Spignesi $9.95 paper (#51776)

What's Your "Mad About You" I.Q.? by Stephen Spignesi $8.95 paper (#51682)

Prices subject to change; books subject to availability